Walking Around in South Street

Discoveries in New York's Old Shipping District

Ellen Fletcher
with a guide to South Street Seaport Museum's ships by **Norman J. Brouwer**

South Street Seaport Museum
in association with
Leete's Island Books

**The publication of this new edition
of Walking Around in South Street
was made possible by a grant from
Furthermore, the J. M. Kaplan Fund
publication program.**

First Printing, 1974
Second Printing, 1975
Third Printing, 1980

Revised Edition, 1999

ISBN # 0-918172-27-6
Printed in the United States.

Leete's Island Books, Inc.
Box 3131
Stony Creek, CT 06405
www.leetesisland.com

Preface

Walking around the streets of the South Street Seaport Historic District today, it is easy to forget that its very existence — much less its excellent state of preservation — is a major miracle.

In 1967, when the South Street Seaport Museum was founded by a group of enthusiastic volunteers wanting to preserve the area and its maritime associations, the New York City Landmarks Preservation Commission was in its infancy. Founded as a response to the, today unthinkable, destruction of the old Pennsylvania Station, the commission was born at a time when "modernization" and "modernism" were still the yardsticks against which real estate development and architecture were judged in this city, a city known for a callous disregard of its past.

Happily we now live in different times. Economic pressure to develop valuable acreage is still a force, but it is increasingly balanced by a sensitivity to the value — both spiritual *and* economic — of what is old.

This district is an outstanding model for the more enlightened approach to development that the city has come to embrace. Designated a landmark district starting in 1968, this neighborhood, far from being hampered by landmark protection, has flourished. The museum has grown and has amassed a fleet of ships that have become familiar — and beloved — icons of the lower Manhattan skyline.

The museum functioned as the guardian of the integrity of the district as it underwent a dramatic transformation in the mid '80s into a "festival marketplace" bustling with shops and restaurants. Under the museum's guidance, two historically appropriate structures were added to the district: the new Fulton Market Building and Pier 17. Both are modern buildings that draw on the vocabulary of an earlier age. More important, historical buildings were stabilized and in many cases restored under the watchful eye of the museum.

The results are plain to the naked eye: block after block of narrow stone-paved streets lined with the eighteenth- and nineteenth-century buildings that once housed the warehouses and countinghouses of a young city's visionary entrepreneurs. What is less obvious to the casual observer is how much the survival of the area as an authentically restored historic district is due to countless hours spent in archives and libraries by museum staff. Chief among them in the early days was the author of this volume, Ellen Fletcher, a tireless researcher, superb historian, and passionate advocate for historic preservation. In this edition, her work has been amplified and updated through the efforts of our current Director of Publications, Madeline Rogers, assisted by long-time docent Paul Brodtkorb, who generously volunteered his time, knowledge, and writing ability. Special thanks, too, to Steven Jaffe, our senior historian and curator and to Charles Sachs, former curator. Their prolonged study of the district, and their scholarly and important contributions to an ever-deepening understanding of South Street's key role in the development of New York, have enriched this already valuable volume.

The republication of this book is long overdue. As with earlier editions, we owe the existence of this revision to the generosity of the Kaplan family — in this case a grant from the Furthermore Foundation, an offshoot of the J. M. Kaplan Fund which has contributed so much to the preservation of the city's heritage.

We are aware that parts of this edition may also need revision in the not-too-distant future, thanks to the burgeoning interest in this old neighborhood, interest that has been accompanied by a burst of development unmatched since the mid-1980s. New residences are being fashioned out of old countinghouses, new structures are rising to fill unsightly empty lots where fire and neglect long ago took their toll.

We hope you enjoy *Walking Around in South Street* and that it will inspire you to explore and re-explore a neighborhood that has so much to teach us about the spirit of this city, the role of maritime activity in shaping our world, and the value of respecting and guarding our history.

Peter Neill
President, South Street Seaport Museum

Introduction

Scoured by centuries of weather and hard use, often out of plumb, the ancient buildings of the Fulton Market neighborhood have a strong character that the passage of time has left them, dropping successive veils of heavy use, change, grime, and neglect over once-crisp brick fronts. The character is there; anyone can sense it, but to understand it specifically, to know the substance behind the illusion, you must look back far into the neighborhood's history.

The twelve-block enclave of warehouses and stores, now a protected historic district with a unique character, has not always been set apart from the rest of the city. Once, when water was the only way to transport people and goods over long distances, this neighborhood was the heart of the commercial city it helped to create.

The South Street-Front Street-Water Street strip on the East River is all "made" land, created between 1686 and 1820 from the tidelands by successive periods of landfill and wharf building. In the nineteenth century, this strip was literally the gateway to the city that lay to the west: Wall Street with its handsome Georgian and Greek Revival buildings — the financial palaces of an earlier day; Broadway with its brilliant retail shops (extravagantly gaslit from an early date and thus open late into the night); and, closer to the East River shipping center, the wholesale shops of Pearl, "the richest street in the city." The name Pearl Street dates to the Dutch colonial days when oyster and clam shells littered tidal mud flats before the landfill began, but later took on a new meaning when the street became the headquarters for the city's most prosperous merchants.

Little still stands of the commercial New York of the nineteenth century — an occasional high-style landmark, well-cared-for, and scattered single and grouped buildings which to varying degrees retain evidence of an early origin. Continued prosperity and the New York characteristic of pursuing progress at the expense of sentimentality and tradition have replaced most of the buildings in downtown New York several times over.

THE SEAPORT 1624-1985

1624
European colonists, sponsored by Dutch West India Company, arrive.

1664
British take possession and rename city and province after James, Duke of York.

1675-1676
Great Dock built between Whitehall Slip and Coenties Slip; only significant place of dockage for large vessels until 1750.

1713
Treaty of Utrecht marks start of major commercial growth for New York.

1719
Gerardus Beekman receives first water lot grant east of Pearl St., between the present Fulton and Beekman streets, on which he builds a public slip.

1

1747-1762
Number of vessels owned by city residents increases from 99 to 447; number of employed seamen grows from 755 to 3,552.

1775-1783
The American Revolution

1784
Empress of China *sails to Canton opening the American China trade.*

1789
Water St. is paved between Coenties and Peck slips.

1793
Peter Schermerhorn consolidates Beekman Slip water lots (later Fulton St. & Schermerhorn Row).

1797
New York becomes leading American port, surpassing Philadelphia's import and export volume for first time.

Front St. is laid out between Beekman Wharf (Fulton St.) and Crane Wharf (Beekman St.).

1807
After trial on East River, Robert Fulton's steamboat North River *makes first trip up Hudson to Albany.*

The dedicated searcher, though, will find his rambles through Whitehall Street, State Street, Pearl Street, Stone Street, Hanover Square, and Wall, Front and Water streets well rewarded when he finds the single and clustered buildings that were houses, saloons, stores, shipping offices, mercantile exchanges, and banks a century or more ago. Several guidebooks are available to direct walkers through the narrow old streets and byways, among them Norval White's and Elliot Willensky's *AIA Guide to New York City* (out of print, but soon to be reissued in a new, updated version by the surviving member of the duo, Mr. White); Gerard R. Wolfe's *New York: a Guide to the Metropolis* (McGraw-Hill, 1993); and Hope Cooke's *Seeing New York* (Temple University Press, 1995), all arranged by district; as well as Ada Louise Huxtable's *Classic New York* (Doubleday, 1964, o.p.), organized by architectural type.

It is after you've pursued the elusive, often hidden old buildings through the narrow streets that the survival of the South Street Seaport district appears all the more miraculous. Here the sun shines at midday into the narrowest streets, the sky somehow seems closer overhead than in the downtown canyons. Here we can see how the city was supposed to look when street widths were determined in the eighteenth and early nineteenth centuries.

To prepare for your walk, think of the days when these streets were first laid out, when land-hungry entrepreneurs pushed lower Manhattan's shores, street-by-street, out into newly minted land claimed from the harbor. If these buildings seem a bit cracked and leaning (notice, for instance, the eastward-sagging lintels over the second and third floor windows of Nos. 4 and 6 Fulton Street), it's because the merchants who built them were in such a hurry to get going that they couldn't wait for their artificial land to finish settling before they framed up their buildings upon new stone foundations sunk into the shifting mud and rubble of the landfill.

Those buildings were, typically, countinghouses. To modern ears, that phrase suggests the Dickensian kind of place where Pip's friend Herbert Pocket worked. Mercantile and multi-functional, a countinghouse might have a store or showroom on the ground floor, with warehousing space in the upper floors. Its name, however, came from its second floor, often reached most conveniently by an exterior iron stairway from the sidewalk to a door on the second floor. Inside were the hand-inscribed ledgers or account books and the several "Herbert Pockets" who did the bookkeeping from which the name "countinghouse" derives.

To get to the beginning of all this, think back for a moment further than these streets themselves, to the first European involvement with Manhattan island. Early in the seventeenth century, even before there were houses here, or a fort, there was the harbor itself and there was trade. We know that at the time of the burning of the Dutch merchant ship *Tijger* in 1614 at least a dozen Dutch ships were using the harbor on trading missions with the Indians. Only the rudest of shelters welcomed the Dutch on Manhattan's shores, but their commercial visits here were many. It is true indeed that New York was a seaport before it was a city.

During the seventeenth century the little outpost grew from a lonely colony in the woods to a respectable commercial town. In 1664, New York became an English colony, its growth fueled by trade and further stimulated by wars with the French over Canada. This early growth — relatively slow and staid compared with what was to come — was interrupted by the American Revolution.

It was after 1783 (the evacuation of the British troops from New York) that the city began to express itself in a startling way. Not a month after the evacuation, merchants were sending out ships on ambitious globe-spanning junkets. The remote commercial outpost was suddenly America's major city. By 1800 the tonnage of its port was greater than that of either Boston or Philadelphia and by 1810 it exceeded the other contenders in population.

New York had just begun to climb in 1800. From then until the beginning of the Civil War, the city, firmly rooted in its mercantile tradition, was what its harbor had made it — and its harbor was ruled by South Street. There, the ruling class of New York, the merchants, could survey from the windows of their tall, proud countinghouses the channel waters and ships lying at anchor along the wharves. Extending inland from South Street were slips and lanes leading, in turn, to Front and Water

1810-1812
South St. becomes city's waterfront from the Battery to former Beekman Slip; Peter Schermerhorn constructs Schermerhorn Row.

1812-1815
War of 1812. Port participates through privateering and shipbuilding.

1816
Fulton St. is named for Robert Fulton (d. 1815). Incorporates Partition, Fair streets, and Beekman Slip.

1817-1825
Erie Canal opens in stages starting in 1820, significantly enhancing port's economy.

1818
Black Ball Line, first regularly scheduled transatlantic packet, begins New York-to-Liverpool service.

1822
Fulton Market opens at Pearl St. and Maiden Lane. East wing becomes fish market.

1835
Great Fire (Dec. 15-16) destroys 674 lower Manhattan buildings.

1838
First transatlantic steam vessels arrive in New York from Britain.

1844-1845
Clipper Ship era opens.
Houqua, *first streamlined
ship, designed for A.A. Low
& Bros. First true extreme
clipper,* Rainbow, *launched
at Smith & Dimon, New
York shipyard (1845).*

1849
*A.A. Low building is erected
on John St.*

1851
Clipper Flying Cloud
*sails between New York and
San Francisco in a record
89 days.*

1882
*Edison opens world's first
central power plant on
Pearl Street. South Street
becomes first commercial
area with electric light.*

1883
*Brooklyn Bridge, under
construction since 1870,
opens on May 24.*

1902-1907
*Chelsea Piers, (800-ft.-
long) docks for largest
ocean liners, constructed
on Hudson River.*

1917
*U.S. enters WW I.
In New York, center for
embarkation and supply,
nearly 1.5 million troops
leave for Europe.*

streets, where the tradesmen and the warehouses (to say nothing of the saloons and boardinghouses) completed the waterfront community.

Following the War of 1812 South Street and New York knew unprecedented prosperity. In January of 1818 the Black Ball Line of Liverpool packets (the first regular transatlantic freight and passenger line) began sailing from South Street just below Peck Slip, near our present Pier 17. "From the sailing of this packet," wrote seedsman Grant Thorburn in his memoirs, "we may date the day whence the commerce of New York began to increase seven-fold." In the 1820s the opening of the Erie Canal channeled farm and industrial produce from the Middle West through New York harbor and out in the city's ships for export. By radically cutting the cost and time to transport goods to and from the interior of the country, the canal made New York the preeminent destination for such goods. Transshipment costs dropped by as much as 90 percent; time was cut by about 75 percent. Until the advent of transcontinental railroads in 1869, other big East Coast ports simply could not compete. Five hundred new mercantile firms were founded in New York in that year alone, but as Robert G. Albion reminds us in his 1939 classic, *Rise of New York Port* (reprinted by Northeastern University & South Street Seaport Museum, 1984), it was South Street, the seaport, that created the canal — that generated the money and the business to build it — *not* the canal that created South Street.

During the second half of the 1820s nearly all descriptions of the city recorded the nearly impassable state of the sidewalks due to mud and the impedimenta of commerce. Crates, barrels, boxes, and carts burst from every overloaded store onto the streets. The 1840s and 1850s saw the zenith of South Street's maritime preeminence. The China trade, led by the merchant firm A. A. Low & Brothers, infused the streets with an exotic glamour that would remain a hallmark of New York culture. Japan had been opened to the West in 1854 and clippers from the Port of New York were carrying thousands of settlers to California. The South Street countinghouses, formerly occupied by one or two firms, began to fill up; sail makers, riggers, figurehead carvers, chandleries, and other waterfront businesses joined the merchants in their buildings.

The heyday soon waned: from the 1860s on, the neighborhood declined in importance. The giant new steamships went to newly built deep-water piers on the Hudson (North) River. The city's commercial center migrated northward, toward midtown. Only the insurance industry around John Street, the investment community centered on Wall Street, and the great shipping firms clustered near the island tip, retained a major presence in lower Manhattan. In and around the old South Street waterfront, raffishness replaced early commercial opulence. As the sailing ships departed, one by one, leaving behind the towers of lower Manhattan — a world-renowned monument to the business they'd brought here — a kind of parochial somnolence began to replace the bustle and world-wide outlook of an earlier age.

Starting in the 1960s, the district, by then a seedy warren of down-at-the-heels commercial buildings anchored by the aromatic Fulton Fish Market, was stirred to new life by the visionary founders of the South Street Seaport Museum. The goals of the museum, officially established in 1967, were both to preserve the district and to acquire and preserve examples of historic vessels that would have been found in the old Port of New York. The historic district's future was further guaranteed when, in 1977, the New York City Landmarks Preservation Commission landmarked eleven square blocks. An additional block was designated in 1989.

Decades later, the founders' perseverance has been well rewarded: The museum they established — now a complex of galleries and ships enlivened with a rich schedule of educational programs — has been designated — along with its partner, The Mariners' Museum (Newport News, Virginia) — as "America's National Maritime Museum." Today the South Street neighborhood stirs to new vitality as an increasing number of its sturdy warehouses are turned into quiet, thick-walled apartments for rent or sale to supply the growing demand for such space by young professionals with families. Tourists pour in as well and the South Street Museum helps bring together visitors, ships, discourse, educational programs, and the reviving bustle of shops and eateries, which has made the area again a cosmopolitan market of goods, of ideas — and of people.

1937
First section of East River Drive completed.

1941-44
U.S. enters World War II and New York becomes nerve center for transatlantic crossings.

1952-53
Third Fulton Market building erected. Approximately 430,000 people work in port-related jobs in New York Port.

1955
Transatlantic air travelers exceed ship passengers.

1960
Water Street buildings demolished for street widening. Contributes to dispersal of old coffee district.

1964-65
Penn Station (1910) is demolished leading to establishment of NYC Landmarks Commission.

1967
South Street Seaport Museum founded.

1975
An estimated 75% of all cargo is containerized; less than 3% of region's jobs are port-related.

1976-1978
Rouse Corp. begins South Street redevelopment.

1983-1985
Redeveloped Seaport opens with dozens of shops and expanded museum programs.

Map One

Begin on Fulton Street on the corner of Front.

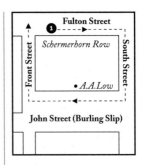

Until blocked off on its western end by the World Trade Center, Fulton was the only street in lower Manhattan to run uninterruptedly from the East to the Hudson rivers, its numbering continuous from east to west. This grandness, though, dated only from 1814 when a new street was ordered to connect Beekman Slip (the present Fulton Street between Pearl Street and the river) and Fair Street (the portion from Broadway east to Cliff Street). In September 1816 the thoroughfare was united under the name Fulton, to honor the inventor and entrepreneur Robert Fulton, who had died in 1815. Fulton was the developer of the steam ferryboat and a major shareholder in the Brooklyn ferry that was launched in 1814 and ran between Fulton Streets in Manhattan and Brooklyn.

While the ferry was active, Fulton Street terminated at the Fulton Ferry house, first a wooden structure of classical design, then a handsome cast-iron building (1863), designed by architect John Kellum and made by Badger's Architectural Iron Works.

As you walk through Fulton Street today you'll notice the pavement of brownish gray stones, each about the size and shape of a loaf of bread. These stones were known as the "Russ Pavement" or "Belgian block" (as the paving type was supposedly a Belgian invention). New England quarries supplied much of this stone — as well as stone for the granite typical of the Greek Revival style, so popular in the 1840s — and shipped it all to the South Street piers in specially designed vessels. Fulton was one of the first New York streets to have its cobblestones replaced by the blocks in 1854.

Schermerhorn Row, 2-18 Fulton Street; 91, 92, 93 South Street; 195 & 197 Front Street

Stand on the northeast corner of Fulton and Front streets. Across Fulton Street stands the Georgian commercial block known as Schermerhorn Row. It was

Map One
From Fulton and Front, east along Schermerhorn Row, south on South Street to John Street, west on John, north on Front back to Fulton.
(Full area map, inside front cover)

◄ **Schermerhorn Row, ca. 1905**
By the time of this rendering, which appeared in *Harper's Weekly*, the Seaport district's glory days were long past. Ships, ferries, and small coastal vessels still tied up at the piers, but the giant oceangoing steamships were using the deepwater Hudson River piers, and the neighborhood had become a somewhat rundown area of small boardinghouses, ship chandleries, and light manufacturing.

A CITY BUILT ON WATER

In an age when most goods moved over water, waterfront land was highly prized. To make more land, the local government sold water lots to private owners with the understanding that they would fill them to create new land for buildings and piers. These so-called water lots were parcels that lay between the marks of high tide and low tide and were therefore under water half the time. To make them usable, their owners had to build them up with landfill, constructing wooden "cribs" to street level which they would then fill with cartloads of earth and refuse. Archaeologists examining this fill have found in it old porcelain, pottery, glassware — broken, cast-off things once used by New Yorkers in the course of their daily lives.

in 1726 that the Schermerhorn family began to buy land in this neighborhood.

Arthur Schermerhorn of the third generation of American Schermerhorns, a shipmaster, purchased land east of Pearl (then Queen) Street from his father-in-law Johannes Beekman in three successive increments in 1726 and 1729. The land was part of a larger grant that had been made to Beekman by the city in 1719.

Two generations later, Peter Schermerhorn the elder, shipowner and merchant (1749-1826), became the family member most active in this neighborhood. Known as "Captain" Schermerhorn, his ships plied the trade routes between New York and Charleston, South Carolina.

During the British occupation of New York in the Revolution, Schermerhorn, a patriot, moved upstate near Poughkeepsie, where his vessels could be kept safe from seizure and where his son Peter Jr. was born in 1781. After his return to New York, he established himself as a ship chandler on Water Street near the Crane Wharf (now Beekman Street).

On December 2, 1793, Captain Schermerhorn consolidated the family water lot holdings (still unfilled) on the south side of Beekman Slip (now Fulton Street) east of Front Street and bought the entire parcel himself. The Taylor-Roberts Plan of 1797 shows this block partially filled and the Bridges Map, surveyed in 1807, shows the entire holding complete, with an alley separating it from George Codwise's land on the south side of the block.

Beekman Slip had not yet been filled, although the Bridges Map, published in 1811, which perhaps shows a projected condition, showed the fill complete. In December of 1813, however, it was selected as the Manhattan terminus of Robert Fulton's Brooklyn ferry for two reasons: first, because by then it actually was filled; and, second — with the joining of Beekman Slip and Fair Street — it provided a direct route to the west side, and, at Broadway, a north-south route, for goods and people coming from or going to Brooklyn and points east.

In 1810, Schermerhorn began to build his block-long row. It was completed in 1812. Although these tall, handsome stores seem more conveniently located and more spacious than the building occupied by the Schermerhorn chandlery at 243 Water Street, the new row was most likely intended as a real estate venture, as the family firm never moved here, and all the stores were leased to other merchants. In 1812 and in 1815 through 1817, however, John Peter Schermerhorn, a son of Peter the elder who had not joined the old firm, ran his own ship chandlery first in the 12 Fulton Street store, then in No. 14.

Peter Schermerhorn had chosen well when he selected the site for his row. In 1793 when he bought his land, the important markets were located to the north at Peck Slip and to the south at Maiden Lane. Hardly had he finished building, though, when the Brooklyn ferry approached him about landing at the foot of his wharf. Because of the ferry, Fulton Street was created and rapidly became one of the busiest in the commercial district. Shortly afterward, a Fulton Market directly across the street became a serious probability. When the market opened in 1822, Schermerhorn Row became one of the most valuable commercial holdings in the city.

The row was built in the conservative late Georgian-Federal tradition then standard for New York commercial architecture. With its brownstone arched doors and wide shop windows, second-story balconies, slate-covered roofs, and rhythmic chimneys, the row was strikingly handsome during its first two decades.

Schermerhorn Row was designed to combine merchants' offices and warehouses under a single roof, representing an early form of an architectural type common to the major seaports on America's Atlantic coast. Its original,

▼ **Schermerhorn Row and Fulton Market, published ca. 1834** When William James Bennett made this view, Schermerhorn Row, on left, was still used for its original purpose, as merchant counting rooms and warehouses. It is the only structure in this view that remains standing today. The first Fulton Market, right, was designed in 1821 by Irish-born architect James O'Donnell, and it opened as a butchers' market in 1822.

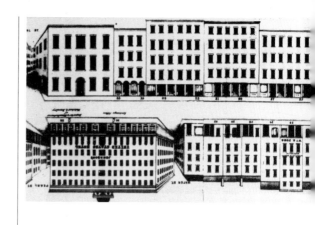

typical ground-floor design consisted of one arched doorway and one standard-sized, double-hung window per building. By the late 1840s many of the old brick fronts had been replaced by granite-piered shopfronts in the Greek Revival style. After another ten years, many were "modernized" yet again with cast-iron columns. All of the row's ground floors have been modified several times in the ceaseless commercial flux which has been its life. Nevertheless, the upper floors, with the exception of one roof change and a few other nineteenth-century alterations, either remain as built or were restored in the 1980s to resemble the row's early appearance.

Look up at the uneven roofline. The **mansard** over 2 Fulton Street and 92 and 93 South Street was added in 1868 to increase the capacity of the steamboat hotel (McKinley's, later called the Fulton Ferry Hotel) that occupied it. Though probably not there when the row was built, the dormer windows and roof hatches atop the rest of the row were added soon after.

Many original details, though partly obliterated, are still visible today. At 2 Fulton Street half of an original arched door surround and the adjacent splayed brownstone lintel hint at the original ground floor treatment. This corner store is shown in the William J. Bennett engraving of Fulton Market, published in 1834 (see previous page). Richard S. Williams, the grocery firm shown in that view, occupied the ground floor store from 1814 until about 1862. It was at Williams's that the Long Island mail was collected from the ferry for distribution by local stages.

mansard roof

A mansard roof has two slopes on each side, with the lower slope steeper than the upper one. The style was popularized in France and named for the 17th-century French architect François Mansart. These roofs came into fashion in America with the Second Empire style, shortly after the Civil War.

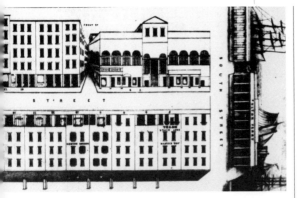

Nearly all of the earliest tenants in the row were clas-
sified as "merchants." Later occupants had varied trades:
grocers, provisioners, eating houses, hotels, liquor shops,
taverns, clothiers, clerks, bootmakers, barbers. Even a
factory later occupied the buildings, tenants making
changes to suit their own needs.

Number 4 Fulton Street has housed eating establishments for more than a century. In 1850 it became Rogers'
Dining Saloon, at which time it boasted splendidly furnished "saloons" on the first and second floors, a kitchen
in the building behind it that fronted on Burling Slip,
and lodgings for boarders on the upper floors. The fond-
ly remembered Sweet's Restaurant was a row fixture from
about 1847 with the opening of Abraham Sweet's "refec-
tory" at No. 8 Fulton — and its expansion in 1864 into
No. 4 — until its demise in December 1992 when it suc-
cumbed to a nor'easter that flooded the neighborhood
and knocked out the electricity for several days.
Basements had to be pumped out; buildings were perme-
ated by the smell of decaying drowned rats for weeks; all
subsurface electrical machinery had to be rebuilt or
replaced; and the remaining Sweet family just didn't have
the heart to restart from ground zero.

Adjacent to Sweet's was Sloppy Louie's, a storied
seafood restaurant, immortalized by the late Joseph
Mitchell in his 1952 *New Yorker* article "Up in the Old
Hotel," which was reprinted as the title story in a collection of Mitchell's work in 1992 (Pantheon). Sloppy
Louie's went out of business in 1998 when Joe Morino,
the nephew of founder, Louis Morino, retired.

JOSEPH MITCHELL

The writings of Joseph Mitchell (1908-1996), many of which first appeared in The New Yorker *magazine, have come to epitomize the Seaport district for many. The republication of Mitchell's work in the book* Up in the Old Hotel *(1992) introduced him to a new generation of fans. In the title story, Louie Morino, the proprietor of Sloppy Louie's restaurant, which occupied the ground floor of the old hotel of the title, reflects on his building's history:* "…the simple fact my building was an old Schermerhorn building, it may sound foolish, but it pleased me very much. The feeling I had, it connected me with the past. It connected me with Old New York. It connected Sloppy Louie's restaurant with Old New York. It made the building look much better to me. Instead of just an old run-down building in the fish market, the way it looked to me before, it had a history to it, connections going back, and I liked that."

Several Schermerhorn Row buildings had upper-floor lodging-rooms in the second half of the nineteenth century. Many of these rooms, though long unused, survive in original condition. The title piece of Mitchell's book gives a classic account of the Fulton Ferry Hotel's rooms above Sloppy Louie's as they appeared in the 1940s.

The South Street Seaport Museum's Visitors' Center and museum shop is part of Schermerhorn Row as well: it is at No. 12 Fulton Street. When the museum's permanent exhibit opens in the upper three floors of Schermerhorn Row, this space will become the main entrance to the expanded museum.

Turn riverward on Fulton Street, then south (right) into South Street.

91, 92 & 93 South Street; lot northeast corner of Burling Slip

Numbers 91-93 South Street, built in 1811, comprise the eastern end of Schermerhorn Row. Originally merchants' counting-rooms and warehouses, the buildings later housed more varied tenants. Nos. 92 & 93 (and No. 2 Fulton Street) were altered and the mansard roof was added, in 1868 when the buildings became a hotel.

At the northern corner of Burling Slip and South Street stood the office of Edward Knight Collins, founder of the Collins line of transatlantic passenger steamships which once rivaled England's Cunard Line. By 1850, Collins ran four splendid steamships: The *Arctic*, the *Baltic*, the *Atlantic*, and the *Pacific*. In that year the *Arctic* sank in a disgraceful accident off Newfoundland, killing 300 people who might have been saved had the crew behaved more courageously. Collins's own family died in the wreck. Next, the *Pacific* simply disappeared and finally Collins was ruined in the Panic of 1857. Plans for this corner call for the erection of a new museum building which will house galleries, reception, and classroom spaces.

Walk into the wide expanse of John Street.

This district and the surrounding neighborhood are home to a number of streets designated as "slips." These were originally exactly that — mamade inlets, lined with wharves where ships could dock to load and unload goods. After they were filled in some, like John Street, were given street names. Others, like Old Slip to the south of the district, retain their original names. Many, including John Street, which is also known as Burling Slip, retain both names.

A.A. Low & Brothers, 167-171 John Street

The silks, porcelains, and especially the teas that filled the holds of the China clippers, were symbols of a glamorous phase of New York's commerce — the China trade. At the pinnacle of the China trade was the firm of A. A. Low & Brothers, founded in 1840 by Abiel Abbot Low, just back from a clerkship in Canton, where he had learned the special practices of the China trade from Houqua, a hong merchant, who was a prominent mentor of young Americans. During its first decade, the firm shared Fletcher Street headquarters with a drug importing concern owned by Seth Low, Abbott's father. In 1849-1850, Low built his strikingly handsome brownstone-faced countinghouse at 167-171 John Street, for which he largely demolished three brick buildings dating from 1811. The Low firm occupied its Burling Slip building from 1850 until after the turn of the century. The cast-iron double storefront is probably original and was made by Badger's Architectural Iron Works, pioneers in the fabrication of cast-iron curtain walls.

The fine old building here before us, set high above a tall basement, has cast-iron piers which once had elaborate Corinthian capitals at the ground floor. When Low's building was finished, Burling Slip was graced with two of the finest waterfront commercial buildings in downtown New York, the other being the large gray building on the opposite side of John Street (Nos. 170-176), erected ten years before, in 1840.

170-176 John Street

Baker, Carver & Morrell, the ship chandlery which operated here until the 1960s, restored the handsome block of granite-faced brick stores built in 1840 for commission merchant Hickson W. Field.

This is probably the only granite-fronted Greek Revival warehouse left in New York's old commercial dis-

THE GREAT CLIPPERS

A great fleet of China clippers was built for the Lows, including Houqua, Montauk, Samuel Russell, Surprise, Oriental, *and* N. B. Palmer, *named for one of the firm's captains. The* Great Republic, *rebuilt after the 1853 fire at Dover Street that cancelled her maiden voyage, also bore the red-and-yellow A. A. Low house flag.*

A. A. LOW & BROTHERS

After Commodore Matthew Perry opened commerce with Japan in 1854, A. A. Low (1811-1893) was one of the first merchants to send ships to the ports of Nagasaki, Shimoda, and Hakodate.

Low was a pioneer as well in where he chose to live. In an era when it was common for businessmen to live near or above their businesses, he commuted on the Fulton Ferry to and from Brooklyn Heights, where his imposing and elegant mansion still stands at No. 3 Pierrepont Place, overlooking the harbor. From his garden and all westward windows, he could see his John Street building and wharves and all of the harbor's profitable activity, a prospect pleasing to anyone, but especially to a merchant prince who owned significant parts of it.

▲ A.A. Low

trict. Never as common as the type with upper stories of brick, this building form, with roots in Boston, was introduced to New York in 1829 by architect Ithiel Town with the silk store of Arthur and Lewis Tappan at 122 Pearl Street. The early nineteenth-century commercial ideal is well expressed in this building: the open colonnade formed by the line of pillars marching across the ground floor façade; the austere gray wall pierced by the rhythmic ranges of dark shutterless windows that gradually decrease in size toward the top floor. When this building was new, its top-floor windows were emphatically shorter than those on the lower floors, typical for Greek Revival buildings. The top floors in this period served either as servants' quarters (in residences) or storage space (in commercial buildings) and architects saw no reason to provide generous amounts of light and ventilation. The short top-floor windows also served an aesthetic function: Because of the foreshortening, when viewed from the street, the structure appears taller. But some later owner of 170-176 John Street must have been more down to earth and needed space that was real, not a mirage, so at some point the tiny top-floor windows — and the upper floor ceiling — were heightened. The alteration is clearly visible where lighter stone was used to extend the façade.

165, 163 & 159 John Street

This site was first built on in 1811 when George Codwise, Jr. sponsored the construction of a six-building row stretching in from South Street, which was later extended to the corner of Front Street. No. 165 was first occupied in 1812 by Merrit & Corlies, flour merchants. From 1830-1835, it housed the offices of metal merchants Anson G. Phelps and Elisha Peck. In 1835 it was the headquarters of Mackie, Oakley & Jennison, commission merchants, who were building the present 181 Front Street. Then in 1839 Edward G. Faile, a grocer, bought the building together with the Front Street corner. He probably altered it in 1840, giving it a Greek–Revival-style ground floor and facing its upper stories in pressed brick. Look today at nineteenth-century doors at the center bay, hung on tapering iron hinges from the granite piers. (Best seen inside the building.)

Turn right into Front Street, walking north.

The buildings on the west side of Front Street in this block were demolished to make way for the One Seaport Plaza tower (Swank Hayden Connell & Partners, 1983), but those on the east side have been restored and developed, together with Schermerhorn Row and the other structures in the block, as part of the Seaport Plan of 1980 — a comprehensive scheme to revitalize the district by transforming it into a "festival marketplace" filled with shops and restaurants. That plan was implemented and the Seaport Marketplace — anchored by the Fulton Market building and Pier 17 — is the result.

189 & 181 Front Street
Built as a pair in 1835-36, these buildings have been joined to their northern neighbor and are now entered through No. 191. The corner building has a sixth floor "classical attic," added in 1917. No 189 was built for Josiah Macy, a shipmaster turned merchant, in 1828. The firm occupied the building until 1885, then moved to 191, where they remained past the turn of the century.

193 & 191 Front Street
The histories of these two buildings are among the most intricate in the South Street neighborhood. Documents show that buildings have stood here since the late eighteenth century; modern structural and archaeological examinations in the 1970s revealed foundations and party walls which suggest the existence of earlier stores. Both of the existing buildings seem to have originally been pitched-roof buildings four-and-one-half stories tall. The façade of No. 193 was probably built in 1877, but most of the internal structure reflects a more recent alteration. Number 191 indicates a major rebuilding around 1860 (when it was purchased by oil merchant W. H. Macy), which left little more than its older side walls standing and gave it the Italianate-style cast-iron façade which is a dominant feature today.

197 & 195 Front Street
These are Schermerhorn Row buildings, described beginning on page 7.

beginning on page 7.

CAST-IRON ARCHITECTURE
Economics dictated the use of iron as a structural element in buildings as early as the late eighteenth century. Iron was not only less expensive than traditional building materials, it also allowed building parts to be pre-fabricated and then assembled on site. In New York, which became the nation's center for cast-iron architecture in the early nineteenth century, the material first appeared as decorative "modern" façades which hung like curtains in front of existing buildings. In the 1840s, one of New York's cast-iron pioneers, James Bogardus, began a campaign for buildings made entirely of cast iron. The idea caught on and many nineteenth-century buildings were constructed this way. The greatest collection of such structures can be found in the Soho and Tribeca districts of lower Manhattan. Cast iron became less prevalent starting in the mid-1880s with the greater availablity of steel.

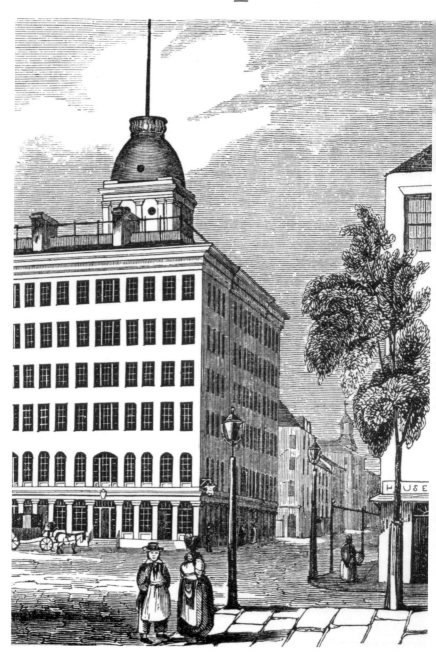

Here you come again into Fulton Street looking north at the modern building at the opposite corner of Front Street.

17 & 19 Fulton Street

Here is a case where the bulldozer got the best that the block-front had to offer. A pair of exceptionally handsome Federal style buildings with arched doorways and balustraded hipped roof formerly occupied these lots. A modern glass and steel building has replaced them, in keeping with the museum's philosophy that new buildings should not pretend to be old ones.

But the new building almost didn't make it either. The plans for this corner were that an old cast-iron building, the 1848 Edgar Laing department store, was to be re-erected here. The store, designed and cast by the architect and engineer James Bogardus in his factory, had been carefully unbolted and dismantled in 1971 at its lot on Manhattan's west side at Murray and Washington streets, to make way for a new building. It was conscientiously stored under the Manhattan Bridge. It was exactly the right dimensions to fit the vacant lots on the northwest corner of Front and Fulton streets. A plaque was to be affixed to the cast-iron building's front, admitting that it wasn't quite *in situ*, but that it was old and wasn't inappropriate for the new site.

The 1983 building that today sits here was erected because when the Manhattan Bridge storage quarters were visited to check on the condition of the Edgar Laing department store, it was missing. Someone had stolen it, and, presumably, had sold it to be melted down for scrap. Plans were hastily revised by the architects, Beyer Blinder Belle, and what was to have been a kind of framework to display (and help hold up) the old cast-iron building became a complete building on its own. The many windows flanked by stylized columns echo similar features of the 1848 store and function, in part, as an homage to the pilfered antiquity.

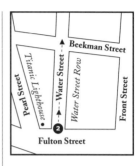

Map Two
West on Fulton Street to Water, north on Water to Beekman.
(Full area map, inside front cover)

◄ **Holt's Hotel**
New York in the nineteenth century was "a paradise of hotels," and the one that started it all was Holt's, erected in 1833 at the corner of Fulton and Water streets. It boasted 225 rooms, a dining room for 1,000 patrons, and the city's first steam powered elevator. Later named the United States Hotel, the building stood until 1902.

GREEK REVIVAL STYLE

In the early nineteenth century, following the Revolution, Americans began turning away from the Georgian-Federal style with its roots in England. Seeking a more American style, they sought inspiration in ancient Greece, identifying with that culture's democratic stystem. The architectural style that evolved — inspired by eighteenth-century excavations of ancient Greek sites — was codified in pattern books from which architects and builders could draw inspiration. The buildings they created or modified were characterized by simple forms and restrained ornamentation.

The Greek Revival style was not favored solely for aesthetic or philosophical reasons; it also had a practical advantage: It allowed builders to install large glass windows on the ground floor so merchandise could be shown by daylight, which was much cheaper than using candles, oil, or gas jet lighting.

21, 23 & 25 Fulton Street

These stores, dating from 1845-46, are late examples of the Greek Revival commercial style. They were built for George W. Rogers. Like the earlier ones, the ground floors here are trabeated granite (post and lintel construction), but look closely at the capitals and see, instead of a molding, a concave profile that is plainer than many of the earlier ones and somewhat Egyptian in feeling. Notice, too, on the west side of the fifth pillar down from Water Street a faint artifact from the past: spelled out in white letters on a faded black background is what might be the word "Agricultural," and agricultural supplies are what were sold there early in the twentieth century. Notice, finally, that the fifth-floor windows are typically shorter than those of the floors below, as are the ones of Schermerhorn Row's top stories and those of the buildings at 170-176 John Street discussed on page 14.

Look west along Fulton Street to the metal and glass skyscraper on the corner of Water Street (Emery Roth and Sons, 1972). When first erected, the developer, Mel Kaufman, graced it with many playful touches. Among them: allegedly the world's largest digital clock (an enormous 72-square "chessboard," whose squares light up sequentially to indicate the hour, minute, and second); dead-pan Pop-Art sculptures on the sidewalk (a bicycle rack and a telephone booth, neither functioning as such); sharp-edged, uninviting metal "love seats"; a huge sunshield over the sidewalk on Fulton. In 1998, this building underwent renovation and is now a dormitory for New York University students who are shuttled to their Greenwich Village campus by chartered buses.

In the nineteenth century, this was the site of Holt's Hotel, which Stephen Holt opened in 1833. Its gleaming marble walls and immense size made it "a wonder of New York," according to a contemporary paper. From its cupola flashed the semaphore signals of one of the city's early "telegraph" stations and it utilized an early if very slow system of hydraulic and steam powered elevators between its floors. Marvelous as this "public palace" was, it was heavily mortgaged and failed, but was reopened in 1839 as the United States Hotel. It stood until 1902 when it was demolished for the building that preceded the Cocoa Exchange on the site, in its turn demolished for what is now there.

Turn right, walking north into Water Street.

The small park at the corner of Fulton and Water streets is anchored by the Titanic Memorial Lighthouse, built in honor of those lost on the *Titanic* in 1912. The memorial originally sat atop the old Seamen's Church Institute building on lower South Street near the Battery. When the building was demolished in 1968, the lighthouse was salvaged and given to the museum.

Try to slice through history to 1720, when the land on your left with the little tree-shaded park between Pearl and Water streets was the eastern limit of Manhattan island. You are standing where the docks of the Cannons, the Livingstons, and the Ellisons jutted into the river behind their Pearl Street buildings. That year, though, these landholders were to erect "a good wharf or street of thirty feet" which was shown completed on the Bradford map of 1731. Water Street was finally widened to its present width and paved with cobblestones as far north as Peck Slip, two blocks from here, in 1788-89.

The block on your right began to be filled by the owners of the water lots granted early in the 1750s and the shore line pushed farther into the river. Little frame houses and houses with brick fronts were common on this stretch of Water Street during the eighteenth century — we find them described in property transfers.

In the late 1820s the character and tempo of Water Street in this district began to pick up. Edmund Blunt wrote in the *Picture of New York or Stranger's Guide* (1828) that Water and Front streets were "occupied by wholesale grocers or commission merchants, iron dealers, or as warehouses for the storage of merchandise and produce of every description." Soon, though, the wholesale grocers and commission merchants were crowded out of the Water Street segment between Fulton and Peck Slip, as that stretch became the undisputed center of New York's stove trade. The whole area was sometimes referred to as "the stove district." In 1840-41 there were nineteen stove dealers here; twenty-nine by 1851. Some occasionally advertised as plumbers. Most dealers supplied various types of stoves, grates, and ranges and offered additional stocks of miscellaneous ironware, tinware, zinc, lead, and

▲ **The Titanic Memorial Lighthouse, circa 1964**
Erected in 1913 as a memorial to those who perished on the *Titanic*, this structure towered 211 feet above the street in its original home at 25 South Street, then headquarters of the Seamen's Church Institute. When the institute moved, the lighthouse was acquired by the South Street Seaport Museum and was eventually moved to its current location at the intersection of Water and Fulton streets. Its most notable feature is a time ball, currently undergoing restoration, which dropped at noon each day to signal the time to ships in the harbor.

*From the seventeenth
through the nineteenth
centuries, New York's
printing industry was
centered near City Hall,
very near the Seaport.
The museum's Bowne &
Co., Stationers is typical of
the thousands of job printing shops that produced
the invoices, coupons, tick-
ets, labels, posters, letter-
head, timetables, and such
that were so necessary to
commerce in a booming
port city. New York, the
financial, commercial,
and shipping capital of
the country, was also the
printing capital. From
1800 to 1890, the number
of printers in the city
jumped from 75 to 8,000.*

copper. All of these items were heavy and most were
coming in by water from upper New York State, or
Massachusetts, or even Europe, so a staging area close to
the wharves of South Street made a great deal of sense.

207, 209 & 211 Water Street

This range of Greek Revival stores is among the best of
the type remaining in New York and it is certainly among
the best preserved. The granite steps, piers, and lintels of
the ground floor are well proportioned and handsomely
tooled. The scoop-troughed rain basins — drainage
ditches cut into the stone paving — that were a practical part of the original arrangement have been restored to
their correct positions. The iron gratings (with wooden
infill pieces added in deference to modern high heel
shoes) originally let a little daylight down to basement
workshops, perhaps helping a cobbler, say, keep his eye-
sight a while longer. Number 211 has the original slip sill
under the large shop window on the left side. Also of
granite is the exceptionally good classical cornice (upper-
most crowning feature) shared by the three buildings.

The brick used in the row's upper stories is harder
and firmer than that of Schermerhorn Row, but not so
hard as the pressed brick used to reface the adjoining 21-
25 Fulton Street buildings. It is laid up in Flemish bond,
a bricklaying technique in which the long side of the
brick alternates with the short end. Flemish bond was
generally out of favor with architects by the 1830s most
likely for reasons of complexity and therefore cost, or
perhaps because the aesthetics of common bond's
unvarying long-sided brick courses seemed more appropriate to the simplicity of Greek Revival, at least in its
Doric mode.

After Ithiel Town designed the granite store at 122
Pearl Street for silk merchants Lewis and Arthur Tappan
in 1829, this trabeated ground floor arrangement became
the standard design for all New York commercial buildings and any mason could build such a store by studying
examples on the streets and in the builders' handbooks.
This row is probably the work of such a mason, possibly
David Louderback, who bought the property at 211 in
1835 and held it in his estate until 1883.

Bowne & Co., Stationers at No. 211, a working job

printing shop as well as a curatorial department of the museum, is based on a nineteenth-century prototype. This building was one of the first preservation projects undertaken by the South Street Seaport Museum, in 1973-74. This project was made possible with financial help and encouragement from the present-day Bowne & Company, still printers and stationers, but now very large, with an international clientele and an expertise in printing governmental and corporate financial records.

213-215 Water Street

Next to the Greek-Revival row, this heraldic Italianate building, displaying the vigor of the cast-iron period, asserts its 1868 construction date high in the pediment above its fifth floor. On the street of stove dealers, and built as the warehouse for a tin and metal company, its deeply modeled façade is of carved limestone above the ground floor, cut to resemble iron. A museum gallery occupies the ground floor of this building and the museum's Herman Melville Library is above it.

Inter City Fish, the yellow brick building on the corner, built in 1914, stretches the full depth of the block, covering the original Livingston water lot grant of 1750. Over recent years, many enterprises, including a multiscreen theater and a women's clothing boutique, have been located here.

Map Three

Charts & Quadrants.

E.M.BLUNT PRINTER,
Navigators Pilots & Charts,
Sextants Spy-glasses &c.

Continue north on Water Street, passing Beekman.

Beekman Street existed here as a narrow dock and alley called the Crane Wharf until 1824, when the street that ended at Pearl was extended to the East River, absorbing the old alleyway. When the wharf became a street, it was widened by removing the buildings that stood until then along its north side. This project was also the chance for the city to do right by the Beekmans, having rebaptized the family's previous street "Fulton." In honoring Robert Fulton, however, the city was inadvertently dishonoring the Beekmans, who were still around and still powerful. Hence the name Beekman Street.

227 Water Street *(also designated 130 Beekman Street)*
Incorporated into an apartment complex in 1998, this is one of those buildings that suffered amputation when the Crane Wharf was transmogrified into Beekman Street. It had been put up as a sail loft for sailmaker Augustus Wright, with plenty of floor space to lay out canvas. When the 1824 alley became a street, its generous Water Street frontage was radically truncated. The Crane Wharf side was demolished, then rebuilt north of where it had been, thereby narrowing the building. This resulted in a curious anomaly: When originally erected in 1798, this was a Federal structure, but Greek Revival was all the rage in 1824. Therefore the Beekman Street side was rebuilt with Greek Revival rectangular lintels above the windows, while those on the Water Street side remain the splayed Federal style of the original. The 1998 conversion has retained this architectural oddity.

229 Water Street

Next door is a ship chandlery built in 1801 in the Federal style. Through later paint you can still see the fine splayed window lintels with their reeded double keystones characteristic of the period. The ground floor,

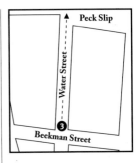

Map Three
North on Water Street to Peck Slip.
(Full area map, inside front cover)

◄ **Water and Fulton, ca. 1817**
This chart and book shop, operated by Edmund March Blunt at 202 Water Street, was one of the hundreds of small district businesses that served the maritime industry.

however, has the plain granite piers of a Greek Revival shopfront, another example of the kind of retrofitting practiced at the time. For builders of private houses and public buildings, the choice of Greek Revival may have had less to do with practicality than with a desire to make a statement through architecture. The implied message was something like this: Our spiritual ancestors were the ancient Greeks, who invented democracy, but were not able to live out that idea. We will be the first country to do that successfully, as our buildings proclaim.

Schermerhorn Ship Chandlery, 243 Water Street

The water lot of William Beekman was divided, and passed out of that family on July 20, 1795. The southern portion was sold to Ebenezer Stevens, a Revolutionary general turned liquor merchant; the northern portion went to Peter Schermerhorn the elder, ship chandler and builder of Schermerhorn Row. The 1795 conveyance mentions that "part [of the property] is made land and the soil under the water to be made..." By 1797 the block had been completely filled and by 1800 Peter Schermerhorn was occupying his new store at 243 Water Street. Apparently the building was not a "store and residence," as was fairly common here in the late eighteenth century, because Schermerhorn, who was well-to-do, was by then living on Broadway. By 1820, though, water records indicate that the building was a boardinghouse, like a number of its Water Street neighbors.

chandlery

A store specializing in the sale of maritime supplies. There were chandleries still doing business in the Seaport district into the 1970s. The largest ones could supply everything from foodstuffs to tools, rope, and canvas for awnings and sails.

Schermerhorn's **chandlery** in its heyday sold almost anything necessary for use on ships. The present façade of 243 recalls its early years, but it is just a mask. Inside, it is an extension of the "new" Seamen's Church Institute building, finished in 1991 (the "old" home was 25 South Street until 1968, with temporary stops at 15 State Street and 50 Broadway on its way here — its most recent home of many — having begun as a chapel on a barge in 1844, or, as sailors often called it, a "doghouse on a raft"). The present building encompasses the lots of Nos. 237 to 243 Water Street. There are no inside party walls, even between 243 and 241 which, from the outside, look like separate structures. The architects (Polshek Partnership) and builders, using the original materials wherever possible, carefully replicated the front of the Schermerhorn

◄ **FLOATING CHAPELS**

*In 1844, two denomina-
tions established floating
churches for seamen right
in the midst of the busy
waterfront. The 1844
Floating Church of Our
Saviour, an Episcopal
church, was a Gothic
structure resting on the
hull of a former ferryboat
at Pike Street on the
East River (shown). In
the same year, a Methodist
organization established
the Bethel ship* John
Wesley *on the Hudson
River at Pier 11, using
the mastless hulk of a
former sailing vessel.
These were the first of
several generations of
waterborne houses of
worship for seamen.
The last was retired in
1912 when the Seamen's
Church Institute opened
at 25 South Street.*

ship chandlery, preserving even its drunken-sailor back-
ward tilt (notice the top of the false vertical join line
between the "two" buildings).

A new, white-painted door has been inserted into a
beautifully preserved brownstone archway with double
keystone lintel. This was the location of a passageway
that used to lead to a wharf and, later, to a spacious courtyard at the center of the block that may have contained
outbuildings. Today, the passageway is sealed, but if the
door did open it would lead only to the cloakroom/recep-
tion desk of the Seamen's Church Institute.

It is worth going through the real door of the
Institute at 241. There you will find an extensive collection of large ship models and a gallery housing changing
exhibitions on nautical themes. The chapel, at the rear of
the building on the ground floor, is a modern masterpiece
and an oasis of tranquility. Visitors are permitted if no
service is in progress. Ask at the reception desk.

The now-sealed passageway between the old 243 and
241 suggests that the structures were originally built as a
pair and the history of the land suggests that a similar
pair may have stood at Nos. 237 and 239. Until 1941,
No. 241 was four stories tall, but its upper two stories and
entire front wall were taken down that year. Above the
ground floor on No. 243's façade remain the fine original
splayed brownstone lintels with double keystones, the
tooling on their masonry still visible. The original
Federal peak roof was replaced by a flat one in 1912.

RICHARD MORRIS HUNT

Vermont-born Richard Morris Hunt (1827-1895) was the first American architect to be Paris trained (at the École des Beaux Arts). Once trained, he moved to New York in 1855 where he founded the Tenth Street Studios and introduced the French atelier system. Among his apprentices was George B. Post, the architect who designed the New York Stock Exchange as well as the more fanciful 211 Front Street. (See page 41). Hunt's best-known surviving designs include the base of the Statue of Liberty, the central Fifth Avenue façade of the Metropolitan Museum of Art, and, in Newport, Rhode Island, two imposing cliffside mansions, including its most famous one, The Breakers, built for one of New York's most prominent families, the Vanderbilts.

245 Water Street

This warehouse was built in 1836 after an older building on the site had been ruined by fire. Although its upper stories were rebuilt and the massively bracketed metal cornice added, it still has the ubiquitous granite ground floor of the 1830s.

No. 245 Water was built for the important copper firm of Hendricks & Brothers, sons of Harmon Hendricks, who had provided the copper sheathing for the wooden hulled *Savannah*, the first transatlantic steamship, and for several of Robert Fulton's steamboats. By the 1830s, when Uriah Hendricks and his brothers took over the firm, their business had shifted from supplying the naval trade to providing copper boilers and other parts to the locomotive industry.

247-249 Water Street

This commercial, four-story, gabled brick and granite Greek Revival building was erected as a warehouse in 1837 for the coppersmith Samuel Thompson. Six large granite piers support a deep architrave which is capped by an unusually ornate cornice. In 1990, after years of neglect, the building was acquired by F. J. Sciame Construction Co., Inc. and was handsomely restored as new quarters for the growing firm. In 1997, seeking larger quarters, Sciame moved to 80 South Street and converted this building into apartments.

251 Water Street

On the southeast corner of Water Street at Peck Slip stands one of the handsomest buildings in the district, built in 1888 by architect Carl F. Eisenach. It was designed with a ground-floor store and apartments for eight families above. Distinguishing the stairway entrance on Water Street is an elaborately cast foliate terra cotta tympanum announcing the street number. The double doors with their massive hinges are probably original. Broad Romanesque Revival arches, which slant outward to meet the ground, frame the ground-floor store on Water Street and Peck Slip. **Terra cotta** lintels above the fourth-floor windows are enlivened by keystones whose haughty faces monitor the business of the street.

257-259 Water Street *(also designated 21-23 Peck Slip)*
Before crossing Peck Slip, look at the six-story apartment building on the opposite corner with the date 1873 in black iron numbers running vertically down its Peck Slip side. It is one of the area's secret architectural treasures. The star-shaped end caps of the numerous iron tie rods between the walls at each floor level, plus the iron shutter-pin hinges beside each window frame, tell us that this was built as a warehouse and a very sturdy one at that. But with its black brick decorative patterns and its handsome proportions it seems more elegant than the typical warehouse. That is because its designer was Richard Morris Hunt, Perhaps the most famous American architect of his period. This building is of special note because it was a departure for Hunt, whose commissions tended to be grand and highly visible.

terra cotta
Much of the elaborate ornamentation on New York City buildings of the late nineteenth and early twentieth centuries is made of terra cotta (fired clay). One of the most famous examples in lower Manhattan is the Woolworth Building (1913) at 233 Broadway. Terra cotta flourished from the 1880s to the 1930s when a taste for elaborate ornamentation coincided with relatively high pay for good stonecutters, and ornamentation of molded, kiln-fired clay was cheaper than sculpted stonework.

Map Four

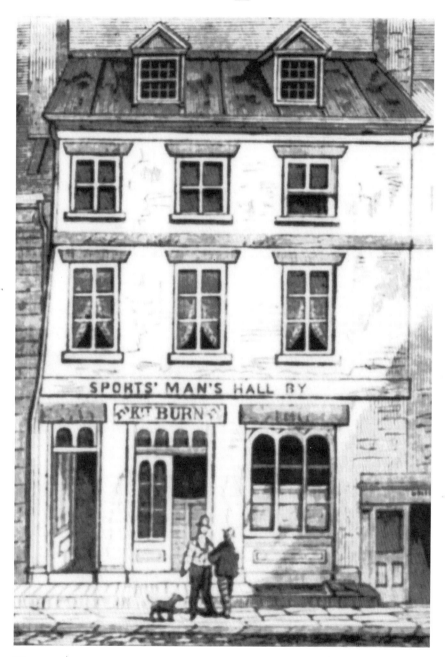

SPORTS' MAN'S HALL BY

K.T BURN

Cross Peck Slip, the site of "Peck's Wharf" in 1730, known by its present name since 1755.

Plans to fill this slip were made before the Revolution, but delayed by war. It was described as "one of the principal wharfs in the city" in 1789, but had been filled in by 1817. At this intersection the city's first brick market was built in 1763 for the convenience of wealthy William Walton and his neighbors on Pearl Street.

261 & 263 Water Street

Built in 1847, these were among the last warehouses built in the Greek Revival mode, their plain piers and unmolded stepped ground-floor lintels representing one of its simplest forms. The original occupants were Thomas Otis Leroy & Co., makers of lead pipe.

265 & 267 Water Street

This eight-story building was designed as a cracker bakery in 1872 by architect Charles Miltain for William Treadwell. Treadwell manufactured hardtack, a nearly indestructible seagoing biscuit, which was delivered directly to the ships at neighborhood piers. If suitably protected, hardtack lasted for years, as it might need to on, say, a whaling voyage. Protection often involved large (almost five-foot-high, -wide, and -deep) riveted iron boxes with manhole cover-like lids, to keep away the ship's rats. (The museum's *Wavertree* has its original hardtack cases on view.)

On the building, many details survive. Original double doors with night shutters survived until recently on the ground floor, and the heavy metal shutters on the upper windows and the modillioned metal cornice are still important architectural features. Iron or steel exterior shutters were an idea whose time, perhaps, never should have come. They were intended to help make buildings fireproof. If a fire broke out, they could be shut, in theory cutting off the fire's oxygen supply. In practice, they tended to cut off not quite enough of its air, grew

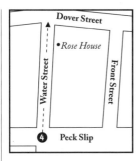

Map Four
North on Water Street, across Peck Slip, continue north on Water to Dover Street.
(Full area map, inside front cover)

◄ **Joseph Rose House, ca. 1866**
This house, built by Joseph Rose, a young sea captain, in 1773 as a residence and shop, was a dance hall and groggery by the time of this 1866 rendering, and had acquired a reputation as one of the "chief citadels of corruption" in an equally unsavory area.

red hot from the fire, passed that heat to the building's wooden framework, igniting the wood, which sometimes led to explosion and collapse.

269 Water Street

The boathouse for the Walton mansion on Pearl Street stood on eighteenth-century Walton's Wharf, now No. 269 Water Street. The nineteenth-century warehouse that replaced the boathouse housed the plumbing establishment of Thomas Dusenbery. He specialized in the manufacture of bath fixtures for residences equipped with indoor plumbing — an innovation made possible (at least for the well-to-do) by the completion of the Croton Aqueduct in 1842, which brought pure upstate water to the city for the first time.

271 Water Street

In the mid-nineteenth-century, No. 271 housed the rag warehouse for the wealthy Cliff Street paper manufacturer Cyrus W. Field (1819-1892), who is best known for founding the company that laid the first Atlantic cable between the United States and Great Britain.

Joseph Rose House and Shop, 273 Water Street

Few buildings are as historically complex as this little brick structure squeezed between its sturdier neighbors. The story begins in 1771, with a real estate advertisement on the back page of the *New York Mercury*. Two lots for sale, it said, already wharfed, on Water Street beyond Peck Slip. Those were troubled days, just before the Revolution, but the city was growing northward. Although the lots were some distance from the busiest part of the waterfront, it was clear the area would increase in value.

A young mariner of Scottish descent, Captain Joseph Rose, bought the easterly of the two lots, on which No. 273 stands today, in October of 1771 and had built a house on it by 1773, a date that makes it the third oldest building of record so far discovered in New York (the Morris-Jumel Mansion in Harlem dates from 1765; St. Paul's Chapel at Broadway between Fulton and Vesey Streets dates from 1766).

Rose and his neighbor William Laight shared a wharf just behind the house where Rose moored his brig,

▲ **Advertisement, 1845**
Thomas Dusenbury's establishment at 269 Water Street was one of many nineteenth-century plumbing and stove businesses conveniently located near the piers of South Street.

Industry. Joseph Rose stayed in British-occupied New York during the Revolution and in 1778 the explosion of a gunpowder ship in the harbor nearby severely damaged many waterfront buildings. The Rose house was fairly close to the disaster. Joseph Rose's neighbor William Laight rebuilt his house in 1780 and since this house once shared a passageway to the wharf with the Laight house, Rose may have rebuilt in 1780 as well.

By 1791 the Rose family had moved to a more fashionable address on lower Pearl Street and this site began hosting a parade of occupants. First Isaac Rose, Joseph's son, ran an apothecary here. In 1812, there was a shoe store on the ground floor and a boardinghouse above.

By mid-century, this section of Water Street had become a neighborhood of boardinghouses, some of them decidedly unwholesome in reputation. Number 273, according to some accounts, was one of the worst. By the 1860s it was a dance house patronized by a resident population classed among "the most depraved and infamous on the entire New York island," its neighborhood called "a slum of moral putrefaction" by the missionary publications of the day. This little building had, by 1868, acquired a reputation as one of the "chief citadels of corruption" in a seamy area, and was the site of "The Kit Burns Dog-Pit," the featured attraction in an otherwise standard groggery. The next year, No. 273 Water Street was chosen by clergyman William H. Boole as a home for fallen women which reportedly admitted about one hundred would-be reformees during its first five months of operation.

A major fire in 1904 destroyed the building's third floor and peaked roof, which was then replaced by third and fourth floors and a flat roof. Another fire in 1976 caused severe internal damage. In 1998 the house was completely rebuilt by the Sciame Development Corp., whose parent company, F.J. Sciame Construction Co., Inc., has renovated other structures in the area, including 247-249 Water Street, south of Peck Slip (see page 27).

Working to a design by architect Oliver Lundqvist and using as much of the structure's original fabric as possible, Sciame created a three-story Federal house based on the only visual record available — an illustration from *Frank Leslie's Illustrated Weekly* showing the house in 1866 when it housed the Kit Burns establishment.

THE WICKEDEST WARD

After 1850, the Fourth Ward, the area of the city just north of the Seaport district, became one of the downtown neighborhoods most associated with crime, poverty, and vice, riddled with cholera, typhus, and smallpox. An 1864 sanitary inspection of the district counted 446 liquor stores and saloons. Drunkenness and prostitution were rampant. One of these establishments was the saloon at 304 Water Street operated by John Allen, dubbed "the wickedest man in New York." In 1868, in an apparent fit of contrition, Allen loaned his establishment to a group of clergymen who held a revival there. Within months, it became apparent that Allen's "conversion" was sham. The district that had been momentarily shaken out of its wicked ways quickly returned to normal and remained one of the city's most dangerous and desperate until the turn of the century.

THE BROOKLYN BRIDGE

At Dover Street you stand virtually beneath the massive pylons of the Brooklyn Bridge, designed by John Roebling and built at great cost and amid unprecedented fanfare from 1867 to 1883. By the 1860s the old Fulton Ferry had reached capacity, but the demand for passage between Brooklyn and New York was increasing tremendously as prosperous merchants moved their families to the suburbs of Brooklyn and Queens.

On May 24, 1883, the bridge opened with a huge celebration. The day culminated in an extravagant pyrotechnic display by the firm of Detwiller & Street.

Before any stones were laid for the first bridge tower, Washington Roebling predicted it would become a national monument and so it is. Despite its international fame, the span belongs most of all to New York and to this neighborhood over which it has loomed for more than 100 years.

The Rose house, now fitted out as luxury apartments, may not look as it did when Joseph Rose knew it, but it does brighten up this borderline glum block and its history is richly expressive of the evolution of Water Street.

279 Water Street

The tradition of hospitality on these premises is a very long one. The original owner was registered as a bottler of wine and porter (ale). Research by historian Richard McDermott has pushed the probable construction date of this house back from 1801 to 1794. On the basis of his findings, the current occupant, the Bridge Café, claims this as the city's oldest continuously operating tavern. It is also the district's only extant wood-frame building. Previous watering holes on this spot have included McCormack's Bar, and possibly the Hole in the Wall, operated by One-armed Charley Monell. An 1847 visitor to the Hole in the Wall would have had to contend with Monell's two barmaid/bouncers, Kate Flannery and Gallus Mag. The latter was said to bite off the earlobes of especially refractory customers, a habit of which Charley was sufficiently proud to keep a jar of pickled earlobes on the bar. Today, a gentler hospitality prevails.

The Walton House, *formerly 326–328 Pearl St. (demolished)*
Just one block inland from the Dover–Water Street intersection, near the place where Cherry, Pearl, and Dover

meet, stood a house which exerted an early influence on this neighborhood's growth. America was still English when merchant William Walton built his Georgian house of yellow brick with brownstone trim in 1752. The family arms, embraced by the richly carved pediment above the doorway, suggested that the Waltons were colonial aristocracy. Gardens stretched down to the East River, and across Pearl Street stood the mansion's stables and carriage house. Accounts of the Waltons' lavish entertainments have come down through the records, including an unusual "wasel frolic" enlivened by "ten sunburnt virgins, lately come from Columbus, Newfoundland."

William Walton had built his mansion well north of the fashionable district and by 1763 he and his neighbors felt the inconvenience of having to travel some distance to a public market. Their petition to establish a new one at Water Street and Peck Slip, where the Long Island farm boats arrived, was approved, and the public market house erected there was New York's first brick market.

In 1784 the Walton House became the first headquarters of the Bank of New York and in 1797 when the bank moved to Hanover Square, part of the mansion became a boardinghouse which slid further from elegance as the years went by. The stately old structure, damaged by a fire in 1853, was finally demolished in 1881, by which time it stood in a run-down district of old shops and tenements.

Map Five

Walk east along Dover Street to the corner of Front.

Several buildings have been lost from this segment of the walk. Their demolition was a sad loss in this neighborhood where every building has its own particular history and character.

Turn into Front Street, heading south.

You are standing in the block where the "great conflagration" of December 27, 1853, broke out in the "Novelty Bakery" establishment of Treadwell & Sons at 242 Front, ruining many of the buildings on this street and on Water and South streets.

More disastrously, the fire burned to the water line the celebrated *Great Republic*, then the graceful queen of the seas, the largest sailing ship in the world. She had been launched just two months before from the East Boston shipyard of Donald McKay and was bound on her maiden voyage to Liverpool. She had been docked at the foot of Dover Street since late November taking on cargo. While on public exhibition at her berth, the *Great Republic* had netted a considerable income by admitting on board around 40,000 spectators who had come to South Street to see her at the rate of twelve and a half cents per person.

At about 1 a.m. on the freezing cold morning of December 27th the bakery fire was discovered. No. 242 Front Street couldn't be saved and by the time the fire companies arrived, the blaze had spread next door. Defying the firemen's efforts, the flames had soon sped through to Water Street, then across to the east side of Front Street and through the block to South Street. From there it was only a matter of time and wind before the news in the "Fourth Dispatch" to *The New York Times* became inevitable: "The fire is still raging with unabated violence... The mammoth clipper, the *Great Republic*, is

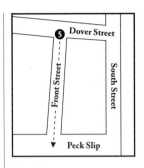

Map Five
East on Dover Street to Front Street, south on Front to Peck Slip.
(Full area map, inside front cover)

◄ **Peck Slip near South Street**
The four-story building on the corner of South Street, No. 151, the Jasper Ward House, now stands alone, its neighbors demolished in 1962.

FIRE!

In the days before New York had a reliable fresh water supply, fire was a constant threat. The problem was compounded by volunteer fire companies, manned by local toughs, who were often more interested in battling each other than in fighting the fire. Though no New York fire was ever as all-consuming as those of the Fire of London (1666) or the Chicago Fire (1871), early New York had its share of devastating blazes. The worst was the fire of December 15-16, 1835, which destroyed 674 buildings on 52 acres in lower Manhattan. But out of the devastating fire came water. Insurance companies lost so much money in the blaze that they added to the growing calls for a reliable fresh-water supply. The result was the construction of the Croton Water system, whose sweet waters began to flow through city taps in 1842.

on fire and will in all probability be totally destroyed!" Still later came the report that heralded her doom: "the masts have fallen and the deck is burning."

The next day, the pyrophile reporter wrote her requiem: "A ship on fire at any time is a grand scene, but the appearance is very remarkable when contrasted with the dark sky of early morning. The falling masts of the Great Republic was a sight than which nothing could be more magnificent."

Under more normal circumstances, this section of Front Street was filled with provision shops of various types: pickle dealers, meat packers, grocers, flour merchants, and bakers predominated during the mid-century golden age of shipping.

259 Front Street

This building — the only old structure now standing on the east side of Front Street — was built for flour merchant David Lydig around 1808. Lydig was one of the "bold race of merchants that built up New York," and had much to do with the proliferation of flour and bread sellers in this area.

Lydig went into business at Peck Slip in 1789, living above his store in the early days. Later he owned a fleet of Hudson River sloops which carried flour, ground at his own mills at Buttermilk Falls (near West Point, New York), to his South Street wharf. With the flour landing at Dover Street, bakers could be assured of a good supply and were encouraged to locate their shops nearby.

His immense success as a flour merchant was due to his exploitation of fast Hudson River transportation. But New York's business climate was changing. Lydig, aware that flour far cheaper than his would soon be coming in from western farmlands via the new Erie Canal, had the foresight to sell his sloops and gradually retire from business as the canal neared completion.

Behind the Lydig building is the spot where the *Great Republic* burned. The rest of the east side of this Front Street block was demolished for the Con Edison transformer station (Edward Larrabee Barnes, 1975), which — with its rhythmic repetition of portals and piers relieving a brick façade — echoes the neighborhood's earlier architectural styles.

242 & 244 Front Street

The west side of the street suffered extensive damage in the 1853 fire and these buildings where the fire broke out were completely burnt and rebuilt. The cast-iron columns on the ground floors are typical of the 1850s and once had bolted-on leafy capitals, now missing. Star-shaped tie-rod washers at No. 242, not uncommon in the district, are attached to the rods that held the building's wood floors to the brick face of the building. At No. 244 handsome iron night shutters survive, barely, at the storefront, obscured by rust. No. 244 is an apartment house, while No. 242 is the north end of The Seaport Inn, its façade and those of the rest of the buildings down to Peck Slip merged together to provide a pleasing old front for a modern hotel.

Passing the scene of the fire, walk on to Peck Slip, named for Benjamin Peck, whose house and wharf were here early in the eighteenth century. Long Island produce boats had docked at Peck Slip long before the establishment of the 1763 market and the site was an important landing for Long Island river traffic through the steamboat era.

Until about 1817, Peck Slip was a waterway open to Water Street and the buildings on either side looked out over the masts of schooners and brigs.

▼ **The Great Republic, 1853**
The great ship is shown here either in New York or Boston harbor. It was on December 27, 1853 that the vessel, the largest sailing ship in the world at the time, burned while taking on cargo at the foot of Dover Street in a fire that started in a nearby bakery.

Map Six

Walk along Front Street south past Peck Slip.

At the time this book went to press the city was reviewing proposals for redevelopment of this sadly decimated block with its gap-tooth appearance — a legacy of years of neglect. Redevelopment will entail erecting some new structures. Buildings currently owned by the city will be awarded to developers for restoration.

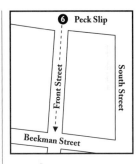

Map Six
South on Front Street from Peck Slip to Beekman Street.
(Full area map, inside front cover)

235 Front Street
The building on the southeast corner of Front Street and Peck Slip, built in 1828-29 for a firm of flour merchants, retains the original Federal-type keystone arch around its Peck Slip door. The rest of its ground-floor façade was remodeled and the peaked roof raised to five stories in 1892 by the fashionable architectural firm of Neville & Bagge, who probably added the pressed-metal window lintels at the same time.

232 & 234 Front Street
Numbers 232 & 234 Front Street, a former double building on the west side, was built under a single street number in 1816. The 234 part of it is now an empty lot, while the 232 side, an apartment house, was completely rebuilt when its sibling fell down or was demolished. In 1816, it was assessed to Gershom Smith, a grocer who had occupied an earlier building on the same site as a tavernkeeper. In 1891, when the front of the building was repaired to correct bulging walls, the building was used as a stable, with carriages on the ground floor, horses conveyed aloft by hoist to the second floor and fodder stored in the loft; but the repair, apparently, was not extensive enough.

226, 224, 222 & 220 Front Street
These buildings on the west side of Front Street occupy an extension of the water lot purchased from William Beekman in 1795 by Ebenezer Stevens (see page 50) and Peter Schermerhorn. In 1797 the wharves were on the

◄ **Fulton Market interior**
The interior of the Fulton Market, which has occupied successive buildings on South Street, was a bustling place in the nineteenth century when the market served both the wholesale and retail trade.

east side of Front Street, and in 1798 Schermerhorn and Stevens built on their Water Street and west side Front Street (220-226) lots. If the buildings on these Front Street lots retain any late-eighteenth-century fabric, it is concealed behind their smooth brick walls and cast-iron storefronts. Like many of the district's oldest buildings, later alterations make them appear to be of late-nineteenth-century vintage.

Both Schermerhorn and Stevens were in maritime occupations (Schermerhorn as a ship chandler and merchant, Stevens as a fleet owner and liquor importer) and finally their two families were joined when John Peter Schermerhorn married Rebecca Stevens. Ebenezer Stevens had been a general in the Revolution and he was elected to the New York State Assembly in 1802. His fleet of ships, which regularly plied the route between New York and the West Indies, included *Gypsey* built by Christian Bergh and the brigantine *Prudence*.

216 & 218 Front Street *(demolished)*

On the side walls of Nos. 214 & 220, flanking the vacant lot, can be seen the "shadows" of the steep pitched roofs of the pair of buildings that stood from 1822 until 1962 at 216 & 218 Front Street. Architecturally superior to their much-altered neighbors, these superb examples of early nineteenth-century commercial architecture could have been the focal point in this Front Street block had they survived.

212 Front Street

Carmine's Bar occupies a corner building erected in 1824, the year Beekman Street was created. This property became a corner lot and the structure, then three-and-a-half stories tall, was built with façades on Front and Beekman streets. The original arched door and window openings in the ground floor on Beekman had brick surrounds with brownstone keystones. These arched openings are reflected in the present stucco-covered arcade at ground-floor level — the arches themselves may exist on the Beekman Street side beneath the covering. The building was raised to four stories in 1890 and the old brownstone windowsills and **lintels** were replaced then with the present bluestone.

lintels

The horizontal elements above a doorway or window. Although functional, they are often decorative as well. In the district, lintels, often made of granite or bluestone, may be simple flat slabs or may be carved or ornamented. The Federal-style double keystone lintel shown is at 229 Water Street (1801). Notice the splayed (angled) corners, usually an indication that a building pre-dates the 1820s.

Return north to Peck Slip and then proceed down the east side of Front Street.

229-231 Front Street

The large warehouse at Nos. 229 & 231, built in 1838-39, has a fine Greek Revival granite shopfront with heavy molded cornice on the lintel and capitals crowning the pillars. The bright hard salmon-colored brick, though its bond is Flemish, appears to be a replacement of the original surface brick.

227 & 225 Front Street

These buildings were built by William Berwick for Peter Schermerhorn in 1822. A close look at the ground floor of No. 225 reveals the tooled brownstone quoins that indicate an original arched opening.

211 Front Street *(142 Beekman Street)*

This corner building (usually designated 142 Beekman Street) is one of the neighborhood's best. With its cockleshell cornice and starfish **tie-rod** ends and its keystones sporting fantastic wriggling fish, the building is jubilantly symbolic of the Fulton Fish Market, which was enjoying a high moment in its history when this structure was built for a Schermerhorn descendant in 1885.

George B. Post, who studied architecture in Richard Morris Hunt's office (see page 26) and was later famous for his New York Times Building (1889) and New York Stock Exchange (1904) as well as the Gothic campus of City College (1903-07), designed this building and its Beekman Street neighbors at Nos. 146 & 148. Its first occupant was fish dealer Samuel T. Skidmore and it has always housed businesses related to the market. During interior renovation several years back, architects discovered an unusual drainage system on the third floor, which is believed to have been built to facilitate the cleaning or preparation of fish. An old fish smoker was also found in the building during its renovation.

At this time, 1999, renovation plans for much of the Front Street block back to Peck Slip are being discussed between the city and various interested parties. What happens or does not happen will depend on many things, most of them controlled by the economy, but any changes

tie-rods

The starfish that adorn the façades of many Seaport district buildings are functional as well as decorative. They are actually the end caps of metal rods that help support the structure. Before the advent of iron and steel framing, buildings were supported by load bearing walls. In commercial buildings, like the countinghouses of the Seaport district, where loads were unusually heavy, tie rods served to reinforce the structure.

Though called a river, the East River is actually a tidal estuary — a body of water linking New York Harbor and Long Island Sound. Its brackish waters — a mixture of salt and fresh — is renewed twice a day as the tide rushes in and then recedes.

made will have to follow the rules of the Landmarks Preservation Commission for designated historic areas.

Look down Beekman Street toward the river.

Today's Fulton Fish Market stands on piles driven into the river's muddy bed. One of the current structures, built in 1907, nearly duplicates in interior plan and function the Victorian wooden structure of 1868 which it replaced. All that's missing are the three cupolas and cruciform peak roofs. A second structure, to the north, was added in 1939.

The Fulton fishermen and merchants were first established on this East River site in 1835, when the city erected for them a wooden shed so they could receive deliveries and make their sales from the same location. Previously, the fishmongers had operated out of the 1822 Fulton Market building, the site of which is now occupied by a modern structure (Benjamin Thompson & Associates, 1983), also called the Fulton Market, between Beekman and Fulton and Front and South streets (see page 47). The fishmongers had shared that 1822 building with grocers, butchers, and cobblers and anyone else who wanted to rent a stall there. But in 1831 the fishmongers were voted out by the others: it wasn't so much the smell of fish, as the water used to clean the fish that contaminated anything it touched, meat, vegetables, baked goods. The wholesale fishmongers decamped and — with the exception of a brief period in the 1840s — have been on the other side of South Street ever since.

When fish came in by boat this was the most practical location possible. But when the old smacks began to be obsolete and the waters of the East River began to poison the fish which had formerly been kept live in the floating fish cars behind the market, some began questioning the wisdom of keeping the fish market on South Street. Rumors continue to swirl about a possible move of the old market to a modern facility in another borough, but for now, the old market is surviving in its historic perch on the edge of the river.

Today the fish are brought in by truck after being offloaded at other piers, or from planes. Nights, from midnight to anywhere between 6 to 9 in the morning, the streets are blocked to normal traffic and it becomes gutter-to-gutter fish here. Then the big cleanup begins in the fish market and the old Tin Building, as the 1907 fish market is called, closes for the day and the tourist buses begin to pull in.

In 1995 the Tin Building burned. The fire started in the second floor, the countinghouse floor, where the business records were kept. City officials had subpoenaed those records to support their contention that organized crime controlled the Fish Market. The fire destroyed the records, but not much else and the market did not lose a day of work. The building was quickly rebuilt to its original appearance and business continues as usual.

▼ The Tin Building
This 1907 structure replaced a nearly identical 1868 facility. Both were constructed on the East River on the site of the first market devoted solely to fish, which opened in 1835.

Map Seven

Continuing south on Front Street, you pass the rear of the Fulton Market block.

It was here on the east side of Front Street that a fire broke out in Sarah Smith's tavern and sailors' boarding-house about three o'clock on the morning of January 24, 1821, reportedly destroying between thirty and forty buildings, mostly wooden houses. Only twelve days before, the city had condemned the block to make way for the planned Fulton Market. The fire burned everything on this side of the block "to a heap of ruins," and endangered the vessels moored at the wharves. All ships, including the sloop of war *Hornet*, were saved by being pulled out into the river beyond the reach of the flames. After this fire, pressure was heavy on the Common Council to begin building, and by 1822 Fulton Market was open. On this side of Front Street was its rear wing, a handsome one-story arcade with a two-story peaked roof pavilion crowned above the center by a cupola.

The west side of the street had many permanent brick structures long before the east side was rid of its wooden shanties. Water lots were granted in the 1750s, Front Street was pushed through in 1797 and that same year the brick houses began to go up on the west side of the street, pushing the wharves out further into the river.

207 Front Street
Number 207 and its neighbor No. 206 are believed to be the oldest buildings on this blockfront and No. 207 may well retain some internal evidence of its earliest form. Like its contemporaries, though, later alterations have left it with an exterior appearance that reflects two centuries of active use. Documentary evidence suggests that a solidly built structure on this site was first occupied in 1797 by Benjamin Stratton, Jr. Internal architectural evidence indicates that the Stratton building was three-and-a-half stories tall and shared a party wall with No. 206. Between 1803 and 1806 Benjamin Stratton, Sr., ran a

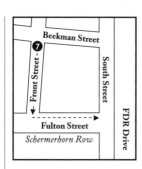

Map Seven
South on Front Street from Beekman Street to Fulton Street, east on Fulton to South Street.
(Full area map, inside front cover)

◀ **206 Front Street**
This lithographic view, made in 1855, shows the building with its original ground floor configuration. The six-panel door opened into a stairhall leading to the living quarters of the upper floors.

boardinghouse here. A jump in the structure's tax value between 1815 and 1816 suggests that a major alteration increased its size as grocers Jonathan and Joseph Coddington prepared to take it over in 1816. At that time it seems to have been raised to its present four-and-a-half story height and extended to the rear, becoming deeper as well as taller. Study of the building suggests that the details of its roof framing may date from the early nineteenth century. The attic still holds the great wooden wheel, about ten feet in diameter, that operated the hand-powered hoisting system. Today, Nos. 206 & 207 Front Street house the administrative offices of the South Street Seaport Museum.

206 Front Street

This building was associated with the Howell family for more than a century. In 1795 Matthew Howell was a grocer on nearby Moore's Wharf. This building, which shared a party wall with No. 207, must have been built during the last three years of the 1790s. Howell occupied it for the first time in 1798 or 1799. In 1814, he changed his business from a grocery to a military store. As dealers in guns and gunpowder the Howells were prominent in the community throughout the nineteenth century. They were apparently the first New York firm to deal in the gunpowder produced by Eleuthère DuPont's powder mills in Wilmington, Delaware.

A lithograph of 1855 shows the Howell store as a fine **Georgian-Federal style** building with separate entrances to shop and residence. By 1880 the building had been damaged by fire and the front wall was then rebuilt, the peaked roof flattened and the present metal cornice added.

205 Front Street

The granite piers of the 1830s at No. 205 represent a major Greek Revival-style alteration to a store built around 1800 for the shipping firm of Jenkins & Havens.

204 & 203 Front Street

Nos. 203 & 204 represent an extensive remodeling in the 1880s that transformed the two buildings, previously separate structures, into a hotel behind a unified façade. The original building at No. 204 dates from 1799, when

Georgian-Federal style
The formal style known as Georgian (after England's royal Georges) was brought to the colonies by English transplants. The style, typified by the use of red brick, simple window and door-frame detailing, fluted or unadorned columns, and symmetry inspired by the ancient Greeks and Romans is often called "Federal" in this country — a name adopted after the Revolution. The style persisted into the 1830s.

it was occupied by Thomas Carpenter, a merchant. No. 203 was built in 1815-16 for Peter G. Hart, a grocer who had occupied a building on this site as early as 1806. Much of the present exterior appearance and most of the structural material, however, including the present storefronts, window placement, running-bond Philadelphia-brick façade, pressed metal cornice, and incised window lintels date from the 1882-83 hotel renovation by Theobald Engelhardt for William Wainwright.

Reaching the corner of Fulton Street, turn again toward the river.

Walk past, on your left, the 1983 Fulton Market building, designed to house a mix of shops and eating places on the site of the original 1822 Fulton Market. The modern 1983 structure replaces a one-story building erected in 1953 half of which was a garage but which nevertheless was called the Fulton Market. Tearing it down was no desecration. It had replaced the 1883 Fulton Market, which had itself replaced the original 1822 Fulton Market. The two earliest markets were important buildings that gave the neighborhood a center. The modern building, with its suspended tin roof canopy echoing the oldest versions of itself, was designed by Benjamin Thompson and Associates for the Rouse Corporation. It is sweepingly spacious and festive when fully leased — a worthy inheritor of its precursors' site.

Cross South Street and stand opposite the center of Fulton, looking west.

You now have the perspective of the Bennett view (1834) of Fulton Street, Schermerhorn Row and the Market (see illustration, page 9). Notice, looking at the illlustration, the neatly flagged sidewalks and crosswalks. The stone was brought from Connecticut quarries and its cool gray contrasted nicely with New York's red brick buildings. Typical canvas awnings, stretched over wood stanchions, created outdoor space for shops in fair weather. The minimal human activity in the view is contradicted by contemporary accounts of shouting hawkers and throngs of people.

WATERFRONT HOTELS
Like all ports, South Street had more than its share of hotels, many of them modest places that could accommodate transients for a modest price; some quite seedy, where down-and-out seamen would bed down. Little is known about the character of the waterfront hotels scattered throughout the district in the nineteenth century, but the one located at 205 Front Street was probably similar to those described by Thomas Butler Gunn in The Physiology of New York Boarding Houses *(1847) as "peculiarly characteristic of the lower part of New York." "A showy bar-room, furnished with the usual amount of plate glass … occupies the front of the lower story. Most of the boarders … are laboring men, having employment in the adjacent wholesale stores, about the wharfs, etc. It is, by express rule, a bachelor establishment."*

Walk north on South Street, past the market block.

Again you pass, on the left, the Fulton Market building. Unlike this building, its earliest predecessor — the E-shaped market of 1822 — was open on the South Street side, its courtyard filled with the stalls of the hucksters and "country people." The 1883 market, more compactly built, had a grand High Victorian façade in dark brick and terra cotta on South Street.

Continue walking north along South Street.

Imagine seeing what a British traveler saw here in 1846: "Massive piles of warehouses line the shores; their long and gloomy terraces, upon the one hand confronting the shipping which becomes denser and more dense as we descend. On the other, the broad quays are covered with the produce of every clime; and barrels, sacks, boxes, hampers, bales, and hogsheads are piled in continuous ridges along the streets, which lead at right angles from the port… The scene is now, in point of activity and animation, beyond all description, whilst the noise is incessant and deafening; the sailor's busy song and the drayman's impatient ejaculation… The vessels which here occupy the slips, are almost all either coasters of the larger class, or engaged in the foreign trade. Passing under their bowsprits, which overhang the footway and threaten the walls of the warehouses with invasion, you pass, one after another, the slips, where lie the different lines of packets … [bound for] the American coastal ports, England, France, the Baltic, Spain and the Mediterranean, the Coast of Africa, India, China, South America, the South Seas, Valparaiso and the Sandwich Islands."

Nineteenth-century descriptions like this one let us glimpse a time and place when commerce had the power to evoke images of faraway places most people would have known only by their products — tea conjured up

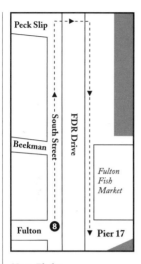

Map Eight
North on South Street to Peck Slip, cross South, south on South Street to Pier 17.
(Full area map, inside front cover)

◄ **South Street in the 1850s**
The sign advertises the Long Island Sound steamers that ferried passengers and cargo between South Street and Hartford, Connecticut.

49

EBENEZER STEVENS

Ebenezer Stevens (1751–1823) typified the merchant shipowners who helped make New York a center for international trade. A war veteran who turned to commerce after the Revolution, his import/export business, based in the South Street district, grew into a family firm, staffed and eventually taken over by his sons. By 1786, he ran a lumber business at 74 Water Street and also shipped American goods abroad. The major source of his income was in the return trade of wine and liquor imports. In 1819, his business moved to 110 South Street. His great-grand-daughter, the novelist Edith Wharton, admired Stevens for "the abounding energy, the swift adaptability and the joie de vivre which hurried him from one adventure to another, with war, commerce and domesticity all carried on to the same heroic tune."

China, oranges Spain, chocolate and cocoa the West Indies. No one who lives in today's environment of television, of easy Internet access to the entire world, of newspaper travel sections and foreign films, could be as affected by the material goods around us as were people who lived in the more insular days of the past.

You see here, past the market block, between Beekman Street and Peck Slip, the last complete block of South Street stores. Dingy now beneath their rusty metal awnings, a century and a half ago they were proud. Banners fluttered from their upper stories, ground-floor ware-rooms were in a flux of activity, merchants barked orders at their clerks from platforms at the rear of second-floor counting rooms. (A few of the counting rooms survived until recently; the imperious platforms commanding the forward part of the floor are easily spotted and certain minor elegancies of trim — a molded baseboard, a stylishly turned column — set them apart from the storage lofts on other floors.)

108-113 South Street

This six-building row was built in 1818-19. Like the Front and Water street buildings directly inland, the southern three were built for Ebenezer Stevens (who used No. 110 in his business) and the northern three for Peter Schermerhorn. Occupied for the first time in 1819 (Nos. 111 and 112 in 1820), this row housed merchants, commission merchants, and grocers. By mid-century, reflecting the trend throughout the South Street shipping community, occupation became denser and merchants made room for block-makers, ship chandlers, cotton brokers, sailmakers, and "forwarders."

Originally four stories tall with peaked-roof lofts, built of brick in Flemish bond, these buildings all had arched brownstone doorways along South Street. At No. 108 and again at 112, the brownstone quoins which defined an original arch can be seen if the ground-floor shutter is up, but much of the visible fabric of the row reflects alterations made after the buildings' original construction date.

115 South Street

Nos. 114 and 115 were constructed together and finished in 1840. The stalwart granite piers at either side are orig-

inal to the building, as is the deep granite lintel above.
The pair was constructed by the prominent mercantile
firm of Slate, Gardiner & Howell, which occupied 115
from 1840 to 1860, when, as Slate & Co., it moved to
114 for its last three years. During the 1880s John J.
Flynn ran a bar and lodging house in the two buildings,
replacing the original center granite piers with the present storefront in 1886. The two-building unit is now
designated only as No. 115.

116-119 South Street
Meyer's Hotel, the handsome corner building on Peck
Slip, was built in 1873 for Long Island attorney William
H. Onderdonk by John B. Snook, the English-born
architect who had designed and built the Grand Central
Depot (1871-72), the precursor of today's Grand Central
Terminal. Snook's original drawings indicate that he
intended the building to be a double store, but after its
purchase by liquor merchant Henry L. Meyer in 1883 it
was converted to the hotel and boardinghouse it

Eastlake style
Charles Eastlake (1836–1906) was an English architect who advocated the use of wooden decoration commonly known as gingerbread. His aesthetic, promoted in his 1868 book Hints on Household Taste in Furniture, Upholstery and Other Details, *was a reaction to nineteenth-century excesses. It became especially influential in this country. The style he championed is characterized by wood construction, decorative wooden planks (or "stick work") which outline the underlying wood frame structure, intricate wooden details, such as lathe-turned spindles, and jigsaw-cut brackets.*

remained until recently. Meyer may have added the diagonal corner entry, with the etched glass panels that still decorate the front doors of the current tenant — the Paris Café — as well as the magnificently flamboyant dark-wood-and-mirrored bar inside, a surprisingly beautiful example of the **Eastlake style**.

Since Thomas Edison was one of the many notables who frequented the place, it is plausibly conjectured that the hotel and its bar were the first in New York to have electric light. The argument might go like this: Edison had finished building his original large direct-current power station four blocks away at 255-257 Pearl Street, between Fulton and John, in 1882; he aggressively marketed the virtues of incandescent illumination; Peck Slip to South Street were within the area supplied by the station; and Henry Meyer, a progressive German businessman converting a substantial building into a new hotel at just the right time in just the right place for this, probably saw the light. Q.E.D., perhaps.

What is more certain is that celebrities as well as Fulton Fish Market workers were attracted to this watering hole. In 1883, right after it opened, Annie Oakley, sharp-shooting star of the Buffalo Bill Wild West Show, threw a party for the brand new Brooklyn Bridge: everyone came. Over the years, visitors have included Diamond Jim Brady, Police Commissioner Theodore Roosevelt, and — more speculatively — Butch Cassidy and the Sundance Kid on their way to South America near the end of their career.

Across Peck Slip, another block of buildings, and one with a distinguished history, stood until the summer of 1973, when all but the two corners were knocked down for the present Con Edison transformer station (*see next page*).

Jasper Ward Store, 151 South Street

At the corner of South Street and Peck Slip, isolated, stands a little four-story building which was once part of a row of three built in 1806 for Jasper Ward, a merchant who occupied the inland building (No. 39, now gone). Ward had purchased the land in 1800, while it was still beneath the water. Shortly after this store was completed, he advertised in the *New York Evening Post* that he had a "Counting-Room, Etc. to Let." The building had "[a] large and convenient Counting-Room on the second story," other floors for storage and it offered "a very excellent situation for a Shipping and Commission Merchant, the store being directly in front of the broad and commodious Pier, the east side of the slip, at which vessels may discharge and take in their cargoes with more convenience than at any other Pier in the city." Merchant Henry Lambert responded to Ward's advertisement and in 1807 he was in business in this corner building. Its soft brick upper stories, laid up in **Flemish bond** and its oddly angled hipped roof are original features, while the granite piers at the ground floor replace a brick façade which probably had the typical arched openings. Above the windows, the cap-molded metal lintels probably replace originals made of brownstone.

Flemish bond

A style of bricklaying in which the long and short ends of the brick are laid in alternate fashion.

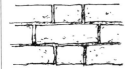

The old building northwards at No. 160 South Street also dates from 1807, a store for flour merchant David Lydig (see page 36). It has been altered.

Consolidated Edison Transformer Station

This power station was carefully planned to complement the historic district, respecting traditional materials and shapes in a modern design which includes a *trompe l'oeil* painting on its Peck Slip side by artist Richard Haas. It shows the Brooklyn Bridge as seen through an arcade, the real thing itself looming above its representation.

Turn around and head south along South Street toward the ships.

As you walk back toward Schermerhorn Row you begin to catch glimpses of the water as you parallel the shoreline of New York. "There now is your insular city of the Manhattoes," wrote Herman Melville in the opening pages of *Moby–Dick*, "belted round by wharves as Indian isles by coral reefs — commerce surrounds it with her surf ... What do you see? — Posted like silent sentinels all around the town, stand thousands upon thousands of mortal men fixed in ocean reveries." The "silent sentinels" are "water gazers ... landsmen; of week days pent up in lath and plaster — tied to counters, nailed to benches, clinched to desks." On any "dreamy Sabbath afternoon,"

— the day and time of the week they are let off from their jobs and all that confines them — they come down to the Seaport to gaze off at the waters of the great port and daydream awhile about far-off exotic lands, adventures, and freedom. This is a scene Melville would have known well. He was born just a few blocks south at No. 6 Pearl Street, shipped out from these wharves, and worked as a port customs inspector.

Today the insular city is "belted round" not only by her wharves, but by the system of highways that girds the lower quarters of the city between the old marginal streets and the river. The elevated F.D.R. Drive has been part of our landscape here at South Street since the early 1950s and unless vehicular traffic in lower Manhattan is curtailed, is likely to remain part of the scene. As you walk down South Street toward Piers 17 and 16, past the old Tin Building of the fish market, the water view is framed through the fretwork of the F.D.R.'s marching stilts and you become inescapably aware, after you reach Fulton Street, of an enormous visual anachronism.

▼ **South & John streets, ca 1890s**
A steamship of the Mallory Line lies at anchor near John Street, far right. The spire of Trinity Church is in the distance.

Cross at the Fulton Street light onto the piers.

The visual shock arises from a jumble of eras: in the water, schooners; a large black bark, its masts looming seventeen stories high, a doughty red lightship, a square-rigger, a diminutive diesel tugboat, all set in front of the tall modern skyscrapers of green glass and steel and beside a festive pavilion of indeterminate age. We are not the first to have been here. Someone had to build New York. Why on earth was it built? The answer lies right here before you, at the meeting of sea and land: Our predecessors built the city *because* of the huge harbor into which it is set.

With its many bays, islands, estuaries, rivers, and nearly eight hundred miles of shoreline, this was early on a "Harbor of Refuge," as a chart might designate it: a place for cumbersome vessels to take shelter behind the bight of Sandy Hook if a gale blew from the wrong quarter. Its complexities invited exploration. Hard-headed, commercially minded captains rode the tide up what is now called the Hudson River in search of the fabulous Northwest Passage to India. The river led to no such mythic passage, of course, but there were, on its banks, native Americans willing to barter furs; and the most militarily defensible landing site became in turn a trading post, a fort, a town, a city. The city's boundaries expanded, sometimes in surprising ways: where we stand was once part of the powerful tidal estuary misnamed the East "River." Once established, the city flourished. From the museum's Pier 16, we can get fresh perspectives on it.

On Pier 16, you will encounter the wooden pilot-house of the tugboat New York Central No. 31. This one-story structure with curved front and overhanging eaves was salvaged from a 1923 Brooklyn-built tug active in New York harbor until the late 1960s: it pushed around barges whose decks were fitted with track to accommodate full sections of New York Central freight trains. The pilothouse is in retirement now and serves passively, as a billboard informing the public about itself and about museum events.

THE STREET OF SHIPS

From 1797 through 1989, New York was the nation's leading port, and dozens of cargo ships, along with crowds of smaller vessels —fishing smacks, coastal schooners, ferries, tugs, lighters, and barges — tied up at these piers, forming a dense forest of masts that stretched two miles from the tip of Manhattan Island north to Corlears Hook. This was the fabled "Street of Ships," center of a world-wide maritime trading economy that turned a handful of New Yorkers into millionaires and created employment for tens of thousands. The arrival of cargo ships akin to Peking *and* Wavertree *would set off a flurry of activity involving scores of businesses and individuals, many located in the small eighteenth- and nineteenth-century buildings that still line the stone-paved streets of the South Street Seaport Historic District.*

Map Nine **South Street Seaport Museum Ships**

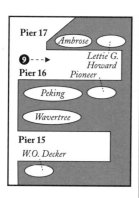

Pier 17
Ambrose
9--->
Pier 16
Lettie G. Howard
Pioneer
Peking
Wavertree
Pier 15
W.O. Decker

As part of its mission to interpret the history of New York as a port city, the South Street Seaport Museum owns the largest privately maintained fleet (by tonnage) of historic vessels in the world. Each of the six vessels tells part of the story of the rise of this great port. The two sailing cargo vessels, Peking and Wavertree, are representative of the kinds of large, sail-powered ships that were the workhorses of world commerce until the dawn of the air age. In its heyday, South Street's piers were lined with ships of this type, forming a dense forest of masts that was as characteristic of the nineteenth-century city as skyscrapers are of today's city. The Ambrose and W.O. Decker are work vessels that did the important business of the port — guiding ships through the treacherous waters of the Narrows and ferrying vessels from place to place. Our two schooners, the Lettie G. Howard and the Pioneer, both traveled the eastern seaboard carrying fish (the Lettie) to market and foodstuffs, raw materials, and manufactured goods (the Pioneer) from point to point.

Ambrose Lightship
Built in 1908

Extreme Length: **135'**
Length on Deck: **134'**
Beam: **29'**
Construction: **steel hull**
Draft: **13'**
Rig: **lantern masts**
Rig height: **67'**
Gross tonnage: **488**

Ambrose Lightship

Lightships were employed as navigational aids where the bottom was too deep or too soft for the construction of a lighthouse. They warned mariners of hazards such as reefs or sand bars, and guided them to port entrances.

The *Ambrose* was built in 1908 to mark the newly opened deepwater Ambrose Channel, which was to become New York harbor's main entrance from the open sea. It was this channel, built from 1899 to 1907, which made possible the giant superliners of the twentieth century such as the *Normandie* and *Queen Mary*. The *Ambrose* greeted these ships at the entrance to the channel until 1936, when she was transferred to the Scotland station off Sandy Hook. She was retired in 1963, and acquired by the museum in 1968 as its first historic ship. Today, the Ambrose station is marked by a tower, and the Scotland station by a giant automatic buoy. This country,

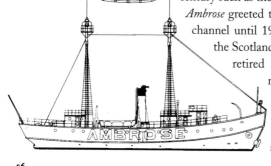

which had over fifty active lightships in the year the *Ambrose* was built, retired its last one in the 1980s.

Lettie G. Howard

This graceful schooner, appropriately moored near the old Fulton Fish Market, is the oldest clipper-bowed offshore fishing schooner left in America. She was built in Essex, Massachusetts in 1893, and originally operated out of Gloucester, Massachusetts, the capital of this country's fishing industry. Her sleek hull was designed to get her catch home to market, while still fresh, from the fishing banks off New England.

She later operated out of Pensacola, Florida, fishing for red snapper on banks off the Coast of Mexico. An engine was added in 1924. The *Lettie* was bought by the museum in 1968 from a group that had been using her as a floating exhibit at Gloucester under the name *Caviare*. For two years, starting in December 1990, her wooden hull was rebuilt, and she was completely fitted out to sail again. She is now employed as a Coast Guard certified sail training vessel.

Lettie G. Howard
Built in 1893 at Essex, Massachusetts

Extreme Length: **129'**
Length on Deck: **83'**
Construction: **wood hull**
Draft: **11'**
Rig: **gaff-rigged schooner**
Rig height: **91'**
Gross tonnage: **52**
Net tonnage: **47**

Pioneer

Pioneer was built as an iron-hulled sloop in 1885, to carry sand from southern New Jersey to an iron works in Chester, Pennsylvania. She later served as a cargo schooner, and then as a small motor tanker, owned in Philadelphia and New Bedford, Massachusetts. She was completely rebuilt with schooner rig in the late 1960s, and given to the museum in 1970. Since then she has spent periods as a training vessel for young people. She currently sails out of the museum's Pier 16 taking paying passengers on harbor cruises.

Pioneer
Built in 1885 at Marcus Hook, Pennsylvania

Extreme Length: **102'**
Length on Deck: **65'**
Beam: **21.6**
Construction: **iron & steel hull**
Draft: **4'6"**
Rig: **gaff-rigged schooner**
Rig height: **79'**
Gross tonnage: **43**
Net tonnage: **37**

Peking

The most impressive exhibit on the South Street waterfront is the giant, steel, four-masted bark *Peking*, one of the largest sailing ships in existence. *Peking* represents the final era in the development of ships using the wind as their sole motive power. She was built at Hamburg, Germany in 1911 to carry cargoes between Europe and the west coast of South America by way of Cape Horn.

Peking was retired from active service in 1931 when a demand for nitrate, her primary cargo, died out with the development of synthetic fertilizers. From 1933 to 1974 she served as a floating school in England's Medway River, with the name *Arethusa*. In 1974 she was purchased for the South Street Seaport Museum to be restored as another example of the latter-day sailing ships whose evolution the South Street Seaport witnessed.

Restoration of the ship's rigging, largely removed in England, was completed in 1998 after twelve years of work by a tiny crew of anywhere from one to three men. Her interiors, also drastically altered, are the process of being recreated to appear once again as they would have when the ship was an active cargo vessel.

Peking
Built in 1911 in Hamburg, Germany by the Blohm & Voss Shipyard

Extreme Length: **377.5'**
Length on Deck: **320'**
Construction: steel hull
Draft: **16'**
Rig: **four-masted bark**
Rig height: **170.5**
Gross tonnage: **3,100**
Net tonnage: **2,883**

Wavertree

The handsome iron-hulled *Wavertree* is a traditional full-rigged ship (square-rigged on all three masts), patterned on her wooden ancestors. She is heir to the tradition of deepwater sailing ships built throughout the nineteenth century for trade in England and America. Ships of her type were a common sight at East River piers from the 1880s until the period of the First World War.

Wavertree was built at Southampton, England in 1885, one of a large number of metal-hulled sailing ships built in Europe well into this century. She was owned in Liverpool, England, and operated in a variety of trades to India and Australia, and North and South America. She called at New York in 1895. Her cargoes included jute, grains, coal, lumber, nitrate, and case oil (kerosene).

Finally, overworked and under-maintained, she was dismasted off Cape Horn in 1910 and sold for use as a storage hulk off the southern tip of South America. She was discovered lying in a backwater of the harbor of

Buenos Aires, Argentina, in 1966. A year later, at the very first meeting of the board of trustees of the South Street Seaport Museum, the decision was made to buy her and restore her at New York as a representative of the ships that called here in the late nineteenth century. She arrived under tow from Argentina in 1970. Since then, the museum has carried out a careful restoration of the ship to return her to her original appearance.

Wavertree
Built in 1885 in Southampton, England for R.W. Leyland & Co. of Liverpool

Extreme Length: **325'**
Length on Deck: **263'**
Beam: **40.2'**
Construction: **iron hull**
Draft: **22'**
Rig: **full-rigged ship**
Rig height: **167'**
Gross tonnage: **2,170**
Net tonnage: **2,118**

W.O. Decker

The wooden tugboat *W.O. Decker* was built in 1930 as the *Russell I* by Russell Dry Docks in Long Island City, Queens, New York. She spent her early years with the Newtown Creek Towing Company, based in the industrial waterway separating Brooklyn and Queens which has its outlet opposite midtown Manhattan. Her original propulsion plant was steam, one of the last installed in a New York harbor tugboat. This was replaced with her first diesel engine in 1947, when she was acquired by the small family-operated Decker Towing Company of Staten Island.

The *Decker* was later based in western Connecticut, where she was used to move fuel barges for a power plant, before being bought in 1977 by museum supporter Geo. Matteson. Matteson berthed the tug at the museum's Pier 15 for several years, continuing to use her for odd towing jobs, and eventually donated her to the museum. She is maintained in operating condition, available for charters and to assist other museum vessels.

W.O. Decker
Built in 1930 in Long Island City, Queens

Extreme Length: **52'**
Length on Deck: **50'**
Beam: **15'**
Construction: **white oak**
Draft: **22'**
Rig: **mast for running lights**
Gross tonnage: **27**
Net tonnage: **1**

Index

(•) description/history